Philippians is my favorite letter from the apostle Paul, and now Dean Flemming's masterful engagement with this gem has become my favorite travel guide to the letter. It is eloquent, perceptive, and relevant to Christians today—just like the letter itself. Philippians is full of joy, community, and (above all) Jesus the self-giving Lord of love. Dean's exposition of it will richly reward any and all who read it.

MICHAEL J. GORMAN
Raymond E. Brown Professor of Biblical Studies and Theology,
St. Mary's Seminary and University

Dean Flemming effectively translates his wealth of knowledge about Paul's letter to the Philippians into a readily accessible guide to its argument. His explanation of self-giving love as the essence of Paul's message accurately captures the heartbeat of the letter's appeal. Having taught Philippians for decades now, I know of no more reliable, theologically informed introduction to this letter than this short gem of a book.

JAMES MILLER
professor of inductive biblical studies and
New Testament, Asbury Theological Seminary

This book is easy to read and understand. It is a cross between a lay commentary and a Bible study, built on Dr. Flemming's in-depth scholarship in Philippians. It is a great small group tool and personal study book, as well as a pastoral resource for preaching on the timely themes of self-giving love, joyful discipleship and community unity.

C. JEANNE ORJALA SERRÃO
professor of biblical literature,
Mount Vernon Nazarene University

In the wonderful biblical epistle known as Philippians, the apostle Paul probes the great mystery that in the self-giving love of Christ the fullness of the nature of God is revealed. Dean Flemming calls this the "V-shaped Story" of God's revelation in this wonderful guide for individuals, small groups, or Bible study classes to use to explore Paul's great letter. The beauty of this road map through Philippians is that it not only helps the reader understand the Scripture more fully, but it helps them know how to enter into the transforming V-shaped story themselves.

T. SCOTT DANIELS

pastor,
College Church of the Nazarene, Nampa, Idaho

The story of Christ's costly, self-giving love that Paul tells in Philippians 2:6–11 is the basis for everything else Paul says in this letter. Using sound scholarship and a warm, engaging style, Dean Flemming takes his readers on a journey through the letter with the ultimate goal of helping them to embody Christ's story in analogous ways in their own contexts. The book is peppered throughout with moving stories of individuals and communities who have done and are continuing to do this, which makes it ideal for small group Bible studies or Sunday School curriculum. It'll be the first thing I recommend to lay readers who are interested in Philippians!

ANDY JOHNSON

professor of New Testament,
Nazarene Theological Seminary

After reading *Self-Giving Love*, I felt that I had just read the fifth Gospel account. But It's not about the life of Jesus as much as it is about how the life of Jesus can be lived out in community. Dean Flemming takes this letter to the Philippians and turns it into a letter to us, the church, as we face pressure from the inside and outside, as we're tempted by success, security, power and prestige. This is a book that shows us how to become the Gospel, how to embody it in skin and blood for a watching world.

DEAN NELSON

journalist and author of *God Hides in Plain Sight: How to See the Sacred in a Chaotic World*

Many writers of a full-size commentary on a biblical book struggle with summarizing its thoughts succinctly in straightforward language. Not so Dean Flemming, despite having written a much longer treatment than this on Philippians! This gem of a little book introduces the reader to the key themes of this wonderful letter of Paul, in easy-to-digest chapters. Practical applications and personal illustrations, including questions for thought and discussion at the end of each chapter, keep the reader's feet firmly on the ground. At the same time, Flemming constantly points us to what in Philippians supports his conclusions, and he writes with a distinguished missionary career behind him that absolutely brims with integrity, service and self-sacrifice for others. If you let it, this book can change your life.

CRAIG L. BLOMBERG

Distinguished Professor of New Testament, Denver Seminary

In a world stuffed with carbo-loaded commentaries, here is the pithy book that pierces to the heart of the matter. Pastorally attuned, missionally sensitive, and keenly perceptive, Flemming's introduction to Philippians delivers the clarity that only arrives on the far side of prolonged study, seasoned by teaching and living with the biblical text. Through Philippians, Flemming takes us into the heart of Paul's theology. At the church potluck of commentaries and introductions, *Self-Giving Love* is the recipe everyone is asking for.

DANIEL G. REID
retired academic editor,
InterVarsity Press

This theological guidebook to Philippians captures the heart of Paul's message to this beloved church: live in and imitate the love of Jesus. Flemming is a wise, warm, and witty companion on the journey to better understanding this rich letter.

NIJAY K. GUPTA
professor of New Testament,
Northern Seminary

SELF-GIVING LOVE

THE BOOK OF PHILIPPIANS

Other titles in the Transformative Word series:

SELF-GIVING LOVE

THE BOOK OF PHILIPPIANS

TRANSFORMATIVE WORD

DEAN FLEMMING

Series Editors
Craig G. Bartholomew & David J. H. Beldman

LEXHAM PRESS

Self-Giving Love: The Book of Philippians
Transformative Word

Copyright 2021 Dean Flemming

Lexham Press, 1313 Commercial St., Bellingham, WA 98225
LexhamPress.com

Print ISBN 9781683594482
Digital ISBN 9781683594499
Library of Congress Control Number 2020946394

Series Editors: Craig G. Bartholomew and David Beldman
Lexham Editorial: David Bomar, Abigail Stocker, Elliot Ritzema,
    Kelsey Matthews
Cover Design: Peter Park
Typesetting: Fanny Palacios

TABLE OF CONTENTS

INTRODUCTION

"Tell me a story!" I can't tell you how many times I spoke those words when I was a child. I directed them to my mom, my dad, my grandmother, my teacher at school—anyone who would listen. These days, my mind still stands on tiptoe when I hear a meaningful, well-told story, whether from a preacher, a teacher, a favorite novelist, or a biblical writer. As human beings, we are wired to love stories. Stories are basic to who we are and how we interpret the world around us. Even in his *letter* to the Philippians, Paul, in effect, tells a story. But this is not just *any* story. For Paul, it is the story of stories, the story that is at the heart of everything God is doing in the world. The story of Christ that Paul narrates in chapter 2 not only becomes a key to understanding the *message* of Philippians, but it also has the potential to shape the character of our Christian lives today. I invite you to join me in listening to the story that emerges from Philippians, a letter that has profoundly enriched and challenged my own life in Christ.

Overview

Paul's Letter to the Philippians has been called a "small gem."[1] Although one of the shortest of Paul's letters, it remains one of the most beloved by the church. Surely this is partly due to the letter's joyful, affectionate tone. In contrast to letters such as 1 Corinthians and Galatians, Philippians addresses a church with which Paul enjoys a warm, enduring "partnership in the gospel" (Phil 1:5). Near the beginning of the letter, he assures these Christians, "God can testify how I long for all of you with the affection of Christ Jesus" (1:8). Paul became this congregation's "spiritual father," founding it on his second missionary journey. But now his situation has changed. He writes this letter from prison, probably in Rome. In part, Paul writes to thank the Philippians for generously caring for him through their representative, Epaphroditus (4:10–20), and to assure them that his present imprisonment in no way hinders the progress of the gospel (1:12–26).

WHERE WAS PHILIPPI?

Ancient Philippi was situated in the northeastern corner of the Roman province of Macedonia (in present-day Greece). It held a strategic position on a major trade route, the Via Egnatia, which linked Rome with the East, as far as Byzantium (present-day Istanbul). Further, the busy port of Neapolis lay only ten miles (16 km) away. These factors made Philippi an important center of trade and travel, both by land and by sea. Acts tells us that Paul first crossed by ship from Asia Minor (present-day Turkey) to the region, in response to a vision of a man from Macedonia (Acts 16:9). Paul headed immediately to Philippi and established the first Christian congregation in Europe. You can read the fascinating story of Paul's early mission in Philippi and the obstacles he faced there in Acts 16:6–40.

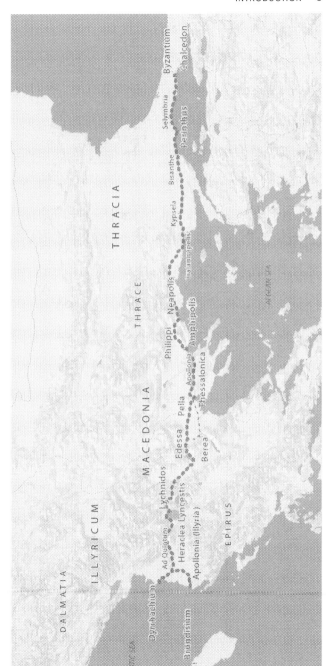

OUTLINE OF PHILIPPIANS

1. Letter Opening (1:1–11)

   a. Greeting (1:1–2)

   b. Thanksgiving and Prayer (1:3–11)

2. Paul's Situation: An Example of Faithfulness to the Gospel (1:12–26)

3. Conduct Worthy of the Gospel: Instruction and Examples (1:27–2:18)

   a. Stand Firm and United in the Face of Opposition (1:27–30)

   b. Practice Unity through Unselfish Humility (2:1–4)

   c. Embody the Story of Christ (2:5–11)

   d. Live Out Your Salvation (2:12–18)

4. Two Christlike Examples: Timothy and Epaphroditus (2:19–30)

5. A Christ-Centered Focus in the Face of Threats to the Gospel: Warnings and Examples (3:1–4:1)

   a. True and False Confidence (3:1–11)

   b. Pressing toward the Prize (3:12–14)

   c. Good and Bad Examples (3:15–4:1)

6. Final Instructions (4:2–9)

7. Concluding Matters (4:10–23)

   a. Gratitude for the Philippians' Gift (4:10–20)

   b. Letter Closing (4:21–23)[2]

This letter, however, is not in the first place about Paul. Above all, Philippians has to do with the advance of the gospel and the formation of a Christian community into the cross-shaped likeness of Christ. As a result, the main part of the letter is saturated with both examples for the Philippians to follow (see 1:12–26; 2:5–11, 19–30; 3:4–17) and instructions to heed (see 1:27–2:18; 4:2–9). At the very heart of these exhortations and examples, we encounter the story of Christ's self-giving love (2:5–11), a story that shapes the character and mission of the church. What's more, Paul brackets the entire letter with a pair of "thanksgiving bookends": he begins and ends by expressing gratitude to his beloved friends in Philippi and thanking God for them (1:3–11; 4:10–20).

The Backstory

Why did Paul write *this* letter to *this* church? Paul's reason for writing Philippians arises not only from his own situation as a prisoner of Rome, but also from the circumstances of the Christian congregation in Philippi. This letter has a backstory, one that Paul likely heard about from the Philippians' messenger, Epaphroditus. Three aspects of the circumstances in Philippi help to shape Paul's exhortations to the church. First, this local congregation apparently faced disagreements and interpersonal tensions within the church (Phil 4:2; we'll say more about this later). Christian unity, then, emerges as an important theme in the letter (1:27; 2:1–4; 3:15). Second, Paul sees a potential threat on the horizon from Jewish Christian agitators (Paul calls them "dogs" and "evildoers"; see 3:2–4). It's likely that Paul was concerned that these teachers might infiltrate the church, bearing a counterfeit teaching that supplemented the gospel by forcing gentile Christians to submit to the Jewish law, especially the practice of circumcision.

Third, the congregation in Philippi met serious opposition from people outside the church. Paul says that the Philippians were engaged in "the same struggle" as he was; they, too, were called to suffer for the sake of Christ (Phil 1:29–30). This harassment most likely stemmed from the Roman populace in their city. Philippi enjoyed the privileged status of a Roman colony. The city functioned like a miniature Rome, outside the capital. In such a setting, loyalty to Caesar and his empire would have been intense. In a city such as Philippi, all kinds of events—including public festivals and meetings of private associations, and even social events such as birthday parties—provided occasions to give honor to the emperor and the local gods that stood behind Caesar. Those who dared to worship a Lord other than Caesar likely would have been considered a threat to Rome and Rome's colony. Consequently, "Christians in Philippi might experience the kind of ostracism, discrimination, or even violence that has accompanied loyalty to Christ in many times and places."[3]

With a missionary and pastor's heart, Paul tailors his reflections on the gospel to the needs and situation of his friends in Philippi. In Philippians, then, we encounter Paul's theological response to his own situation and that of a congregation facing pressures from both inside and outside the church (see 1:27–30; 4:2–3). The result is a Christ-centered letter that continues to shape communities of Christians today.

The Theological Center of Philippians

Philippians has a theological nerve center. It is found in the V-shaped story narrated in the hymn-like passage in Philippians 2:6–11. In this story, Christ, who is equal with God, makes himself nothing, taking on the form of a human being. The story plunges to its lowest depth when Jesus humbles himself to the extreme. In obedience to God the Father, he dies a disgraceful death on a cross. At this point, the story suddenly veers upward (the second part of the V). In response to Jesus' costly obedience, God exalts him and gives him the divine name of Lord. The narrative reaches a glorious climax when all creation confesses that Jesus Christ is Lord, to the glory of God the Father.[4]

From one perspective, Philippians 2:6–11 narrates the gospel that Paul wants the Philippians to embrace, proclaim, and live out (1:27). It gives us a thumbnail sketch of God's gracious, loving activity on behalf of people and the whole of creation in Christ. But, in Philippians, Paul doesn't tell the V-shaped story of what God has done in Christ simply to inform our belief system. He describes Jesus' downward descent so that God's people will reenact that story of self-giving love in their own circumstances. We are to "have the same mindset as Christ Jesus" (2:5).

Philippians, then, spotlights the downward path of the V-shaped story. The story of Jesus humbling himself and pouring himself out for others, even to the point of death on the cross, is not only the source of our salvation; it is also the pattern of our lives. New Testament scholar Morna Hooker hits the nail on the head in noting that the direct link between theology (who God is and what God does) and ethics (what we should be and what we should do) is one of the signature contributions of this letter to the church.[5] For Paul, both the good news and our Christian life, which flows out of the gospel, are cruciform—shaped by the cross. For Christ-followers, as well as for Christ, the way up is down.

The good news story of Philippians 2:5-11 assures us, then, that Jesus is both Lord of all and the pattern for life in conformity to Christ and his cross. Reading Philippians forces us to ask how this story of Christ's self-giving love might collide with other popular stories in our cultures— controlling stories of upward mobility, success, security, and power. Paul's portrait of God in Christ in Philippians, therefore, speaks loudly to the church today.

Using This Book

When I am traveling, I often use a guidebook. It helps me to know where to focus my attention, gives me background information, and explains things about the area I wouldn't have known. Even when I'm roaming familiar territory, a guidebook helps me notice things I never saw before. Sometimes it spurs me to explore a place further on my own or with my travel companions. Think of this book as a kind of travel guide. Whether Philippians for you represents familiar ground or a new adventure, I hope that this guidebook will help you hear this letter in a fresh way, through the lens of the V-shaped story of Christ. In order to get the most out of the journey, I encourage you to do the suggested readings and reflect on the questions at the end of each chapter. My hope is that you will allow the magnificent story that Philippians tells to shape and transform you, even as it continues to change me. So let the journey begin.

SUGGESTED READING

☐ At the beginning of this study I encourage you to read the whole book of Philippians, from start to finish, preferably in one sitting. It won't take as long as you might think. Look at the big picture of the letter. Try to see how it all fits together.

Reflection

After reading Paul's Letter to the Philippians, what are your initial impressions of it? What did you notice about Paul's relationship with his readers?

_____

_____

_____

Reflect on one way that stories have helped to shape your own way of thinking and living.

_____

_____

_____

What might having "the same mindset as Christ Jesus" mean for you and your Christian community?

_____

_____

_____

2

A PORTRAIT OF GOD IN CHRIST

What Is God Like?

Some time ago, I heard a story about a five-year-old girl who was drawing enthusiastically on a sheet of paper. Her mother noticed and asked her, "What are you drawing, dear?" The little girl confidently shot back, "I'm drawing a picture of *God!*" Trying to gently correct her daughter, the mother replied, "Honey, nobody knows what God looks like." Without looking up from her work, her daughter announced, "They will when *I'm* finished!"

One of the most important questions asked by Christians (and many non-Christians) is: What is God like? Paul's Letter to the Philippians addresses that question by drawing a robust portrait of God. This gracious God is on a mission to redeem humanity and restore all things in Christ (see 2:10–11). It is God who brings about our salvation, from start to glorious finish. Paul confidently declares that "he who began a good work in [or 'among'] you will carry it on to completion until the day of Christ Jesus" (1:6). In the present, God is at work among

his people, empowering them to work for his good plea-
sure (Phil 2:13). In the end, God will restore his loving sov-
ereignty over the whole creation. By the power given to
him by the Father, Christ, at his return, will "bring *everything* under his control" (3:21). God's restoring purpose is
good news for creation, as well as people.

God's lordship and providential care form the bedrock
of the entire letter. God is working out his purposes in
Paul's imprisonment (1:12–26). Both believing in Christ
and suffering for Christ are gracious gifts of God (1:29).
God is the one and only source of righteousness—a right
relationship with God and others (3:9). God extends mercy
to his faithful servants (2:27). The "God of peace" is present among his people (Phil 4:9), guarding their hearts and
minds in Christ (4:7). The letter crescendos to a rousing
climax with the promise of God's lavish generosity and
care: "And my God will meet all your needs according to
the riches of his glory in Christ Jesus" (4:19). Considering
all this, our only fitting response is to give "our God and
Father ... glory forever and ever. Amen" (4:20; compare 1:11).

The Self-Emptying God

Only in the V-shaped story of 2:6–11, however, does
Philippians' portrait of God come into sharpest focus.
This poetic passage narrates the journey of Christ Jesus,

> who, though he was in the form of God,
>   did not regard equality with God
>   as something to be exploited,
> but emptied himself,

> taking the form of a slave,
> being born in human likeness.
> And being found in human form,
> he humbled himself
> and became obedient to the point
> of death—
> even death on a cross.
> Therefore God also highly exalted him
> and gave him the name
> that is above every name,
> so that at the name of Jesus
> every knee should bend,
> in heaven and on earth and under
> the earth,
> and every tongue should confess
> that Jesus Christ is Lord,
> to the glory of God the Father. (NRSV)

The story begins in the lofty heights of heaven, with Christ, who shares the glory and exalted status (literally, "form") of God; in other words, "equality with God" (2:6). These opening phrases describe the divine majesty and position of Christ before he became a man.

But then the story starts to careen downward. Jesus refused to exploit his exalted status for his own advantage. Instead, he "made himself nothing" (2:7) when he took on our humanity. The verb Paul uses here literally means that he "emptied himself." Throughout the centuries, Christians have asked questions such as, What did Jesus *empty* himself *of* when he became a man? Some speculate that Jesus laid aside his divinity, or perhaps his divine qualities, such as his knowledge, power, or omni-presence, when he was born in a manger in Bethlehem.

Paul, however, seems to have little interest in such questions. Rather, he defines Jesus' self-emptying in terms of what Jesus *took on*. In truth, Christ "got into our skin," embracing the human situation in all its lowliness and humiliation. He exchanged "the form of God" for "the form of a slave" (2:6–7 NRSV). In Paul's world, slaves were people with no rights; they enjoyed little or no status in society. Jesus, then, not only became human, but he iden-tified with the lowest of the low and the poorest of the poor, the rejected and the marginalized. He came all the way down to where we are.

But the story plunges even lower. Jesus humbled him-self even to the point of "death on a cross!" (2:8). This is shocking stuff for Paul's audience. Crucifixion repre-sented the ultimate instrument of terror, torture, and shame in the Roman world. It was a punishment reserved for those with no status, such as rebellious peasants, hard-ened criminals, and lowly slaves. In fact, so many slaves died by means of crucifixion, it became known as the "slaves' punishment."[6] Jesus not only took on the lowly status of a slave in his earthly life, but he also died the death of a slave on a Roman cross. You simply can't go any lower than that! The contrast with Jesus' supreme status and glory in the first part of the hymn couldn't be more striking. This is the amazing depth of divine love![7]

Suddenly, however, the V-shaped story takes a dra-matic turn upward. Paul announces, "*Therefore* God exalted him to the highest place" and gave him the name of *Lord*—the divine name, which is used to speak of God in the Old Testament (Phil 2:9–11). Here we encounter one of the clearest affirmations of Jesus' divinity in Scripture. Paul paints Christ in bold colors as the exalted, sovereign, reigning Lord of the universe, before whom every knee will bow "in heaven and on earth and under the earth" (2:10). But the passage makes it clear—and this is a crucial point—that Christ is exalted as Lord of everything precisely *because* he emptied himself and humbled himself and died a slave's death on a cross (2:6–8). This means that Jesus' servanthood and self-giving love are as much a part of his divine identity as his exaltation in heaven. The story of Jesus emptying himself as a human being did not represent some temporary step away from his true character as God—like a film star who puts on a disguise so that she can avoid being recognized in public. Rather, it enables us to see what God is really like. "Christ came from the summit of divine glory to die the death of a slave—because such limitless love expresses what it means to be God."[8] Theologian Karl Barth points out that when ancient Christian artists picture the exalted Christ, enthroned in heaven, we still see the wounds of the cross on his hands and his side.[9]

If we want to know the identity of God, we can't begin with a prepackaged list of God's attributes—his omnipotence, his omnipresence, and so forth—and then try to squeeze Jesus into that template. We need to look to Jesus himself, who reveals God's identity to us. If we want to know what God is like—God is like *Jesus*. Jesus' *actions*—his refusal to take advantage of his divine status, his embrace of human weakness, his cross-shaped love—uncover the true character of God. Philippians reminds us

AUGUSTINE ON THE POWER OF PARADOX

Listen to these moving reflections on the paradox of Jesus' incarnation and death from the early church father Augustine of Hippo. I urge you to read it out loud:

"What greater mercy is there than this, which caused to descend from heaven the maker of heaven; which reclothed with an earthly body the one who formed the earth; which made equal to us the one who, from eternity, is the equal of the Father; which imposed "the form of a servant" on the Master of the world—such that the Bread itself was hungry, Fullness itself was thirsty, Power itself was made weak, Health itself was wounded, and Life itself was mortal? And that so that our hunger would be satisfied, so that our dryness would be watered, our weakness supported, our love ignited. What greater mercy than that which presents to us the Creator created; the Master made a slave; the Redeemer sold; the One who exalts, humbled; the One who raises the dead, killed?"[10]

that self-emptying is more than a one-off action. It is the nature of a God who relates to humanity with an amazing love that gives itself away.

This was critical knowledge within the status-obsessed Roman world in which the Philippians lived. Rome also told stories. Rome's story promised to bring salvation and peace to the empire's subjects. But it only did so by means of self-glory, raw power, and violence. God, in contrast, fulfills his saving purpose for humanity through self-giving and death on a cross. The two narratives couldn't help but collide head-on, like trains barreling toward each other on the same track. The story of a Lord who "made himself nothing" turns the Roman value system of what constitutes true status and power upside down. For those who live in a culture that is obsessed with heroes and winners, that collision of stories seems every bit as real today.

So What?

What, then, does Philippians' portrait of God and Christ mean for people like us? For the vast majority of people in our world, the critical question is not, "Does God exist?" but "What is God like?" It's not enough to say, "I believe in God." It makes a monumental difference *what kind of God* we believe in.

Not long ago, a small crack began to develop in the lens of my cell phone. I took numerous photos with my phone before I even noticed it. When I looked at those photos, however, I discovered that this tiny distortion in the lens carried a major impact. Everyone and everything looked slightly hazy and out of focus. It wasn't until I had the lens repaired that my photos once again came into sharp focus.

Unfortunately, many followers of Jesus carry around a flawed understanding of God, which in turn distorts how they picture their whole lives and all of their relationships. For example, some Christians picture God as a heavenly parole officer, who is waiting for them to mess up in some way, so that he can throw the book at them. The result is often a life of guilt, frustration, and fear. Others envision God as a kind of celestial Santa Claus (or Father Christmas, depending on where you live), a kindly grandfather-type who dispenses presents to people when they are nice. Such a picture can easily produce a flabby form of Christianity, which expects God to reward us for our good behavior and to protect us from any hardship or suffering. Still others imagine God as a distant despot, someone living in "a galaxy far, far away" (for you Star Wars fans). This is a God who's nice to believe in, even to pray to when I'm stuck with something I can't handle, but who doesn't hold much influence over how I live my everyday life on earth.

The V-shaped story in Philippians 2 shatters such feeble and misguided understandings of God. It reveals a God who is like Jesus, a God who reveals himself in the humility of self-emptying and in the weakness of the cross. Philippians beckons us to refocus our fuzzy image of God. We need to see God as someone who identifies with the least and the lost of humanity, who stands with us in our suffering, whose character is self-giving love, and who calls us to conform to that character as well. How we answer the question, "What is God like?" makes all the difference.

SUGGESTED READING

☐ Philippians 2:6–11

☐ Philippians 3:20–21

☐ 1 Corinthians 1:18–2:5

Reflection

In your experience, what are some of the most common pictures of God that people hold today?

_____

_____

_____

How do you typically tend to answer the question, What is God like? How does your own picture of God compare or contrast with Paul's portrait of the self-emptying God in Christ in Philippians 2:6–11?

_____

_____

_____

In the Roman world of Paul's day, Jesus' shameful death *on a cross* would have shocked and disgusted people. Are people still shocked by the symbol of the cross today? If not, how might we help contemporary people recapture some of the shock connected to how far Jesus went to save us?

_____

_____

_____

_____

3

PAUL'S STORY AND THE STORY OF CHRIST

My grandmother was a master storyteller. I never tired of hearing her stories. Some were tales she made up as she went along—stories that captured my attention and ignited my imagination. My favorite stories, however, were stories she told from her own life and the lives of her parents. Through listening to her recount these experiences, I discovered who she was, what she valued, and, perhaps most importantly, whom she worshiped and served. But I was also drawn *into* these stories that were part of my family heritage. They began to shape *me*, as well.

In Philippians, Paul not only tells the story of Jesus. He also narrates his own story. In fact, he does so repeatedly in the letter (see 1:12–26; 3:4–14; 4:11–13). These autobiographical passages don't simply give us a portrait of Paul; they also serve as examples for Paul's readers, including us. In many ways, Paul's story mirrors the story of Christ. Paul's identity and mission make no sense apart from his intimate relationship with Christ, so that's where we'll begin.

Knowing Christ

Philippians shows us an apostle obsessed by Christ. Paul testifies, "For to me, to live is Christ" (1:21). His consuming passion is "the surpassing worth of knowing Christ Jesus my Lord" (3:8). The great goal of his life is to know Christ in a full and final sense (3:14). For Paul, knowing Christ involves entering into the story of Christ. We encounter one of the most powerful testimonies in all of Paul's letters in Philippians 3:10–11. Paul writes: "I want to know Christ—yes, to know the power of his resurrection and participation in his sufferings, becoming like him in his death, and so, somehow, attaining to the resurrection from the dead."[11] Paul's desire to "know Christ" isn't a matter of simply knowing *about* him, but rather knowing *him* in an intimate, profoundly personal way. You might know the pope, for example, in the sense of knowing *about* him--his personal history, his character, his beliefs, his accomplishments. But that is quite different from the kind of intimate, experiential knowledge you might share with a long-time spouse. It's this knowledge of deep personal relationship with Christ that Paul unrelentingly pursues.

Paul had first come to know Christ years before as a result of his earth-shattering encounter with the risen Jesus on the Damascus Road (see Acts 9:1–19). But, for the apostle, that profound experience was not simply a distant memory, like a museum artifact to be admired from time to time. Paul discovered that the knowledge of Christ was an inexhaustible fountain; there was always more of Christ yet to experience. For Paul, the "surpassing worth of knowing Christ" far outshone everything he once relied on and held dear (Phil 3:3–8). New Testament scholar Lynn Cohick summarizes well Paul's message for the Philippians and for us: "no earthly love, worldly passion, time-bound desire, or acquired privilege can begin to compare to the ongoing relationship that is ours in Christ to enjoy."[12]

Paul goes on to unpack further what knowing Christ entails. It involves sharing in Christ's suffering and death, as well as his resurrection, both now and in the future (Phil 3:10–11). It is noteworthy that Paul puts the desire to know the power of Jesus' resurrection *before* the participation in his sufferings. Although this reverses the *chronological* order of Jesus' death and resurrection, according to Paul's *theological* calendar, it makes good sense.[13] Without the power and vindication of the resurrection, our present suffering has little meaning.

What, then, does it mean to *know* the power of Christ's resurrection? Paul is speaking of *God's* power—the very power that raised Jesus from the dead! Paul sees the life-giving, resurrection power of God as the ongoing experience of those in relationship with Christ. Elsewhere, Paul connects God's power to the Spirit's work within, which enables Christians to experience in greater measure the love of Christ and the fullness of God's presence in their lives (Eph 3:14–21). This, however, is not simply a one-sided, triumphal message. Paul reveals a magnificent paradox, one we cannot afford to miss. We can experience Christ's resurrection power only if we are willing to share in Jesus' suffering and death. In fact, the passage tightly binds knowing the power of the resurrection and the fellowship of Christ's suffering, like flip sides of the same coin.

Paul uses a word here (the Greek word *koinōnia*) that speaks of an active and intimate "participation" in Christ's sufferings. What kinds of sufferings? Most likely, Paul primarily has in mind the experience of hardships and persecution that he and other believers faced because of their loyalty to Christ and the gospel (see Phil 1:29; 2 Cor 1:5; Col 1:24). Once again, Paul's story is woven into Christ's story. Knowing Christ involves deeply identifying with a Christ who endured suffering for others. When Paul suffers on behalf of Christ, he shares in Jesus' very life and experience.

The thought extends further with the phrase "becoming like him in his death" (Phil 3:10). This doesn't refer specifically to martyrdom, but rather to the daily practice of living out the cross-shaped story of Christ. Even as Jesus' journey to the cross was a way of humility, suffering, and self-giving love (see 2:6–11), so it will be for his followers. If we truly know Christ, we will become like him. The more we identify intimately with a Christ who became "obedient to death—even death on a cross" (2:8), the more we will reflect his likeness.

But this isn't the end of the story. The goal of knowing Christ intimately lies in the future, when Paul shares in the final resurrection from the dead (3:11). Paul's present experience of Christ's resurrection power (3:10) is incomplete. It's a foretaste of the full revelation of that power in the end, when God raises all those who are in Christ and makes all things new. Later in Philippians, Paul joyfully anticipates the return of the Lord Jesus Christ, when the bodies of Christians are transformed to be like the body of Christ's glory (3:20–21). For God's people, resurrection is both a present reality and a future hope.

The exemplary role of Paul's own story in Philippians signals that he wants his readers to enjoy the same intimate, growing, transforming knowledge of Christ that he experiences. And that means becoming like Christ in *both* the weakness of his suffering and death *and* the victory of his resurrection. Unfortunately, Christians all too often elevate one side of this tension and downplay the other.

When I lived in the Philippines, I noticed that images of the suffering or entombed Jesus played a prominent role in the popular consciousness of the culture. For example, the iconic statue of the Black Nazarene represents a suffering Jesus carrying his cross on the way to the crucifixion. Every year, the statue is led through the streets of Manila in solemn procession, surrounded by millions of devotees. Such portrayals of Jesus profoundly resonate with people who face daily physical and economic hardship. But if we *only* emphasize Jesus' suffering and dying, we can easily miss the joy and victory of Easter. Filipina theologian Melba Padilla Maggay pleads, "We need to make the emphatic transition from the cross to the empty tomb! Failure to do so consigns our people to the subtle demonic lie of seeing the work of Jesus, and life itself, as an endless passion, a picture of eternal defeat and unrelieved tragedy."[14] Paul's vision of the Christian life is far more robust than simply muddling through our troubles and trials, apart from Christ's resurrection power and the Spirit's enabling.

For Christians in the West, the greater danger remains a one-sided focus on the victory of Christ's resurrection, without conforming to his cross. As a result, "popular preaching and theology too often promise power without weakness, success without suffering, prosperity without sacrifice, salvation without discipleship, religion without righteousness."[15] This is what theologian Dietrich Bonhoeffer labeled "cheap grace," and Paul would have none of it. Philippians calls us to embrace the *whole* story of Jesus. To know the power of Christ's resurrection, we must travel the way of the cross.

Prisoner and Proclaimer of Christ

Paul's life in Christ is inseparable from his calling as a minister of the gospel of Christ. Paul writes this letter as a prisoner of Rome (Phil 1:7, 13–14, 17). Apparently, Paul stands under a capital charge, which could cost him his life (1:20–23). But these adverse circumstances in no way prevent his fruitfulness as a servant of Christ. To the contrary, what's happened to Paul only works to advance the gospel (1:12). On the one hand, Paul's imprisonment directly under Caesar's nose has enabled the good news of Christ to penetrate into the bloodstream of Roman imperial power. Paul rejoices, "It has become clear throughout the whole palace guard and to everyone else that I am in chains for Christ" (1:13). On the other hand, Paul's faithfulness under fire serves as an example for other Christians to courageously share the good news (1:14).

Paul's commitment to the progress of the gospel also trumps the personal attacks of other Christians.[16] Apparently some other Christian preachers, motivated by personal rivalry, took advantage of Paul's imprisonment to try to discredit him (Phil 1:15–18). Paul, however,

PAUL'S CHAINS

Repeatedly in Philippians 1, Paul refers to his "chains" (1:7, 13, 14, 17). This language may constitute more than simply a figurative way of speaking about imprisonment. It was common for Roman prisoners to be manacled to the soldier guarding them. This fits with Luke's description of Paul's Roman imprisonment in Acts 28. Acts indicates that Paul remained under a soldier's guard, probably chained to his wrist (Acts 28:16, 20).

doesn't let such unjust treatment rob him of his joy. He says, in effect, "As long as Christ is still being preached, I'm willing to lay down my own rights, even my wronged reputation. The greater good of the gospel comes first!"

This doesn't mean that bad motives from those who bear witness to the gospel are inconsequential. After all, a few verses later, Paul exhorts us to live "in a manner worthy of the gospel" (Phil 1:27). Paul doesn't excuse self-ish motives in Christian leaders, and neither should we. But Paul is confident that God is big enough to use even an imperfect and insincere witness to the gospel for his great purposes. At the same time, Paul's response reminds us that the gospel takes priority over the need to defend ourselves. When I am falsely accused or my motives are questioned, my first inclination is to defend my rights. I want to expose those who oppose me. But there are times when setting the record straight is less important than the advancement of God's mission in the world.

For Paul, the ministry of the gospel isn't limited to preaching the good news and planting new churches. He is also deeply committed to forming communities of growing and mature disciples (Phil 3:12-16), Christians who are conformed to the character of Christ (2:1-11). Faced with the possibility of martyrdom, he is even prepared to forgo his personal preference to depart this life and be with Christ (Phil 1:23). Like Christ himself, he puts the interests of others before his own. His ongoing ministry among his friends in Philippi will result in their "progress and joy in the faith" (Phil 1:24-25).

Living the Story of Christ

Throughout this letter, Paul's own life becomes a living demonstration of the story of Christ. This is clear from the start. Paul introduces himself not as an authoritative apostle, but, literally, as Christ's *slave* (Phil 1:1). This striking image spotlights Paul's lowly, loving service to Christ. What's more, it holds special significance within the Letter to the Philippians. Paul is the slave of the one who took "the form of a slave" (Phil 2:7 NRSV). Paul follows his Master in embracing the humble status of a slave.

Likewise, in chapter 3, Paul's own history echoes the story of Christ, unfolded in Philippians 2:5-11. Paul begins by describing his former high position and privileges in Judaism (3:4-6). His pedigree was stellar, his zeal unsurpassed, his performance without a black mark. But, like his Master, he renounces his elevated status. All that he once valued, including his own righteousness, Paul now considers as utter loss, no better than garbage (3:7-9; see 2:6-7), compared to what he has found in Christ. As we have seen, he shares in the obedient suffering and death of his Lord (3:10; see 2:8). In the end, he hopes to participate in Christ's resurrection from the dead (3:10-11). For

SLAVERY IN THE ROMAN WORLD

Readers of Philippians today might find it rather startling that Paul calls himself and Timothy *slaves* of Christ (Phil 1:1). For many people today, the word "slave" conjures up images of the demeaning, race-based institution of slavery that plagued the history of the United States, among other lands. It may also trigger thoughts of brutal kidnappings of children or the tragic trafficking of women, which produce modern forms of enslavement throughout our world.

Slavery in Paul's world was more complex. The practice was deeply entrenched in the Roman Empire. As many as one in three persons living in the cities of the Empire at the time were slaves. Unlike the slave experience in North America, slavery in the Roman world was not based on race, and slaves came from a wide range of socioeconomic backgrounds. Slaves were not always oppressed; at times they even could hold positions of high responsibility in a household. Nevertheless, masters could treat their slaves with harshness and brutality, and often did. It's all the more remarkable, then, that Paul reaches for this metaphor to describe his relationship to Christ. Perhaps no other image could speak so powerfully to people in his world of Paul's exclusive loyalty and obedience to his Lord, as well as the humble, servant character of his ministry.

this reason, he presses on toward the ultimate prize, for which God has called him heavenward (3:14; see 2:9–11). Although the parallel isn't identical, Paul's testimony of his own experience in 3:4–14 cannot help but remind us of the journey of Christ. Paul embodies the same V-shaped pattern of going down, suffering, and being raised. Paul's personal narrative, then, offers a compelling example of cross-shaped living for the Philippians, and for us, to follow (see 3:17).

Here we see a marriage of theology and biography.[17] In Philippians 3:4–14, one of Paul's richest statements of the gospel of God's grace in Christ comes to us in the form of personal testimony. Paul's own life becomes a proclamation of the good news of Christ's death and resurrection, salvation by God's grace through faith (see 3:9), and the reality of being united with Christ. Such an interweaving of theology and biography should characterize our lives, as followers of Christ, as well. People are unlikely to be impressed with our most cherished doctrines, such as justification or sanctification, unless they see that theology lived out in skin and blood. We can never be content to give lip service to our theology unless it is translated into living, breathing biography. My father was a pastor, and I heard him preach every Sunday when I was growing up. However, I learned my greatest lessons about the power of the gospel from Monday to Saturday, as I watched him respond to unjust criticism, or when I saw him embody a life of self-giving love in our home.

Enabled by Christ

Philippians 4:11–13 offers another example of Paul's life reflecting the story of Jesus. In the midst of thanking the Philippians for their practical, financial support, Paul reflects on his own situation. "I have learned to be content," he testifies, "whatever the circumstances" (4:11). What do those circumstances involve? Paul talks about being in need, experiencing hunger, and living in want, as well as having plenty (4:11–12). Once more, Paul reads his own story in light of the story of Christ. He is willing to be humbled, lacking even the basic needs of life, just as Jesus "humbled himself" in obedience to the Father (2:8).

The word for being "content" in this passage (4:11–12) was sometimes used by the philosophers in Paul's world for living self-sufficient lives. They taught that through rigorous self-discipline and inner strength, individuals could become masters of their own universe. Their goal was to become so independent from outward circumstances that they could remain blissfully unmoved by anything life tossed their way, even, say, the death of a spouse. Paul's concern, however, takes a vastly different focus: not *self*-sufficiency, but *Christ*-sufficiency. "I can do all this through him [Christ] who gives me strength" (4:13), Paul exults. Paul doesn't face painful circumstances by building up his spiritual muscles. Instead, he has learned in the school of contentment that *he* does not have to be strong to cope. Elsewhere he testifies, "When I am weak, then I am strong" (2 Cor 12:10). Paul understood that true contentment comes only when we give up our need to be strong.

Unfortunately, well-meaning Christians regularly take Philippians 4:13 out of context, perhaps as much as any single verse in the New Testament. "I can do *all things* through him who gives me strength" morphs into everything from a self-help pep talk to the battle cry of an underachieving church league basketball team! But for Paul, doing "all this" through Christ's strength refers to discovering a God-empowered contentment amid all the ups and downs of life.

How we hear this word is shaped by our life circumstances. African theologian Eshetu Abate observes that these are challenging words for Christian communities who daily face poverty, social upheaval, violence, epidemics, and natural disasters.[18] Other Christians must discover the meaning of contentment in the midst of affluence, when there is always the temptation to crave a bit more. Furthermore, material success can entice us to depend on ourselves, rather than God. We need God's enabling power as much in a time of prosperity as one of poverty. Whether we find ourselves dining on crumbs or caviar, whether in suffering or success, Christ alone remains our strength.[19]

Rejoicing in Christ

Not only does Paul testify to Christ-enabled contentment, but he also exudes *joy* in Christ. Over and over, Paul bears witness to the practice of rejoicing (Phil 1:4, 18; 2:2, 17; 4:10). This is the same apostle who suffers as a prisoner of Caesar under a capital charge, who even faces "friendly fire" attacks from other Christian preachers (1:15–18). For Paul, Christian joy doesn't depend on pleasant circumstances or outward success.

In chapter 2, Paul draws on a stunning image from the practice of ancient sacrifice. He is willing to be "poured out like a drink offering" on behalf of his friends in Philippi (Phil 2:17). In the Old Testament, animal sacrifices frequently were supplemented with a "drink offering" that was poured on top of the sacrifice (see Num 15:1–10). Here Paul says, in effect, "I am the secondary drink offering that is being poured out on the main sacrifice of *your* faith." Whatever being poured out might entail for

Paul—hardship, imprisonment, suffering, even death—he can still rejoice, because it will result in the faith and obedience of others. Once again, Paul models before us the life of self-giving love, following the one who was obedient even the point of death on a cross (Phil 2:8).

At the same time, Paul urges his readers to join him as "fellow rejoicers" in the face of opposition (2:18; 3:1; 4:4). Indeed, joy in the midst of tough times becomes a keynote of the entire letter. Then and now, such joy is only possible because it flows out of a deep and abiding relationship with Christ; it is joy "in the Lord" (3:1; 4:4).

SUGGESTED READING

☐ Philippians 2:12–26

☐ Philippians 3:1–14

☐ Philippians 4:10–15

☐ 2 Corinthians 4:7–12

Reflection

Which is easier for you to identify with and experience—the power of Christ's resurrection or the participation in his sufferings (Phil 3:10)? Why?

_____

_____

_____

_____

What are some of the things that you have had to consider as a loss for the sake of knowing Christ (Phil 3:7–8)?

_____

_____

_____

_____

How difficult is it for you to learn to be content, whatever the circumstances (Phil 4:11)? What is your typical response when you are faced with adversity?

_____

_____

_____

_____

4

LETTERS AND EXAMPLES

Philippians as a Letter

I may be stating the obvious, but Philippians is a *letter*. That means that we will be disappointed if we come to Philippians looking for a detailed account of Jesus' earthly life, death, and resurrection, as we find in the Gospels. Nor will Philippians offer us a historical narrative of the early church, such as we encounter in Acts, or the kind of end-time visions that characterize the book of Revelation. Rather, letters such as Philippians are written out of a concrete situation of the author to specific congregations in their real-life circumstances. They address the particular needs and challenges faced by a local Christian community, seeking to encourage, warn, correct, and instruct converts in the way of Christ.[20]

In one sense, Paul's letters function as stand-ins for what Paul would say to a given congregation, were he there in person. Paul's letters, then, become instruments of his missionary work. Ultimately, a letter such as Philippians is a *community-forming document*. It's intended to shape a congregation of believers in Jesus into a mature, missional community of faith, within its life circumstances.

But that raises a question. If Philippians is written to address the issues and challenges faced by a first-century Christian congregation in the ancient city of Philippi, does that make it somehow less relevant for *us*—people who live in very different circumstances today? The over-whelming testimony of Christians through the centuries, including our own, has been that texts like Philippians are able to transcend their own specific time and place in history. For one thing, we discover many similarities between the congregation in Philippi and churches in various cultures and settings today—churches that still wrestle with the threat of disunity, churches that struggle to remain faithful in the face of opposition and trying circumstances, churches that are tempted to follow other loyalties than the gospel, or other lifestyles than the way of Christ.

Beyond that, as Christian Scripture, Philippians bears witness to a God who still calls his people to experience an intimate and joyful knowledge of Christ, to be trans-formed into the cross-shaped likeness of Christ, and to tell and live the gospel of Christ in their world. This first-century letter, then, speaks a compelling word to people like us. Yet readers of Philippians must remain sensitive to the tension between the letter's mooring in its first-century context and its enduring message for every generation and culture. To read Philippians faithfully, we cannot ignore either of these horizons.

The Letter Form

Just as today's letters follow a fairly consistent form (Dear
_____, ... Sincerely, Dean"), so it is with ancient letters.
That formal structure commonly takes this pattern:

- a salutation (A to B, greetings)

- a health wish to the recipients or, less frequently, a thanksgiving to the gods

- the body of the letter, which contains its main
  theme and purpose

- a closing, which usually includes a both a wish
  for the recipient's well-being and a farewell

Paul typically follows this basic form. However, he
adapts it for his own theological and pastoral purposes.
Here's how it looks in Philippians:

- letter opening (address and greetings; 1:1-2)

- thanksgiving (1:3-11)

- body (1:12-4:20)

  - body opening (1:12-26)

  - body middle (1:27-4:1)

  - body closing (4:2-20)

- letter closing (greeting and blessing; 4:21-23)[21]

Paul's opening thanksgiving section (1:3-11) offers a
prime example of how he transforms the normal cultural
conventions of ancient letters in light of the gospel. As I
just noted, letters in Paul's world often included a prayer
for health or a thanksgiving to the gods, or both. We
see this in a letter written in Greek from a man named

Apion to his father, Epimachus: "Before all else, I pray that you are well and that you may prosper in continual health. ... I give thanks to the Lord Serapis because, when I was endangered at sea, he rescued me."[22] Paul, however, expands this customary practice and charges it with a powerful theological current. Three noteworthy differences stand out. First, rather than giving thanks for health, safety, or good fortune, Paul expresses gratitude for the Philippians themselves. Second, Paul joins his thanksgiving with an intercessory prayer for the church. Third, Paul uses his thanksgiving to introduce some of the key themes of the letter (e.g., joy, partnership/sharing, the gospel, the grace and glory of God).

Learning from Paul

Christians today can learn from Paul's practice of creatively transforming cultural conventions in the service of Christ.[23] We, too, must discern how to draw on the cultural resources available to us in order to tell and live out the liberating good news in fresh ways. For example, Christians in the Majority World, as well as in increasingly postmodern contexts in the West, might need to supplement traditional word and reason–based communication of Christian truth with more visual and artistic forms of expression. Likewise, Christian communities today may need to learn the language of metaphor, story, and symbol, which speaks so powerfully to many contemporary people. For my students, story lines and characters from popular movies often provide points of contact for communicating biblical truth. Whatever our life circumstances, we must learn to sing the old gospel story in new keys.

Philippians as Rhetoric

Paul wrote letters such as Philippians within a largely oral culture. What's more, Philippians was addressed to a *congregation*, not simply to individual Christians. Paul's words were intended in the first place to be heard out loud in a house church setting, rather than read silently. In such a public setting, Philippians would have assumed the character of an oral sermon to a community of believers.

This oral dimension to Philippians encourages us to examine it in light of the patterns of ancient *rhetoric*—the art of persuading an audience. Rhetoric was highly valued in the Philippians' Greco-Roman world. In fact, popular orators who could capture and win over an audience with their persuasive skills were the rock stars of the day. They would have shattered the competition on *Philippian Idol*! As a good communicator, Paul regularly draws on rhetorical conventions of the time. It only makes sense that he would do so. Attention to rhetoric would have helped to enable what he wrote to carry persuasive impact for his audience. Understanding something of Paul's use of rhetoric helps us to see how the letter works to further Paul's goal of bringing about transformation in the lives of the Philippians. Two aspects of ancient rhetoric are worth considering at this point.[24]

Arguments

Long before Paul wrote letters, Greek philosopher Aristotle spelled out three types of persuasive arguments, based on three crucial elements in human communication: the speaker, the audience, and the message. We encounter all three of these types of persuasion in Philippians.

First, arguments from *ethos* draw on the credibility and character of the speaker or writer. In particular, Paul uses this kind of appeal in his autobiographical sections, when he tells his own story (see 1:12–26; 3:4–14; 4:11–13). Paul, for example, claims that his "chains" as a prisoner have served to advance the gospel (1:12–13).

A second type of argument, known as *pathos*, appeals to the emotions of the audience. For example, Paul's expressions of deep affection and care for the Philippians are drenched with *pathos* (see 1:7–8; 2:16–18; 4:1). How could the Philippians fail to be moved by an expression such as this: "My brothers and sisters, you whom I love and long for, my joy and crown, stand firm in the Lord in this way, dear friends!" (4:1)?

Third, arguments appealing to logical persuasion, or *logos*, feature in Philippians, as they do in all of Paul's letters. In chapter 2, for example, Paul urges God's people to work out their own salvation, with fear and trembling (2:12). He then immediately gives their work a basis and anchor in God's prior work among them (2:13).

Examples

One of the most prominent forms of persuasion in Philippians is the appeal to *example*. Ancient orators and philosophers often presented their audiences with examples of lives worth imitating. Sometimes they recalled their own life story, as a means of moral instruction. Paul uses this strategy extensively in Philippians. He points young Christians to lives that are worthy of following on the journey of living faithfully before God. Both Paul and the philosophers of the day understood that truth is often better *caught* than *taught*. The big difference, however, between Paul's use of examples and that of his contemporaries is that Paul connects every human example to the supreme model of Jesus Christ. Jesus himself provides the ultimate pattern of faithful obedience in the face of suffering. And the story of Jesus becomes the template for humility and self-giving love for others. God's people are to "have the same mindset as Christ Jesus" (2:5).

Every other exemplary story Paul tells flows out of the story of Christ. In chapter 2, for example, Paul spotlights two of his colleagues: Timothy, who puts the interests of others ahead of his own (2:20–21), and Epaphroditus, who has risked his own life in order to offer practical service to Paul (2:29–30). Furthermore, Paul appeals to his own history as a concrete example of a life patterned after the cross-shaped story of Jesus (3:4–14). Then, to ensure that the Philippians don't miss the point, he makes things quite explicit in Philippians 3:17 (compare 4:9): "Join together in following my example, brothers and sisters, and just as you have us as a model, keep your eyes on those who live as we do." Such a statement might strike us today as a case of someone who thinks a bit too much of himself. But remember that when Paul says, literally, "Imitate me," this only has meaning in light of Paul's conforming to the self-giving pattern of Christ. In another letter, Paul urges, "Follow my example, as I follow the example of Christ" (1 Cor 11:1). Furthermore, Paul understood well that young believers within a pagan culture desperately needed concrete examples of what it meant to live out the gospel in everyday life. We might imagine Paul as a master craftsman, who mentors an apprentice by first demonstrating how to work with gold or silver, then encouraging the trainee to follow his lead.

Unlike the Philippians, we have the New Testament to instruct us in how to live. Nevertheless, the gospel is still often communicated as much by lives well lived as by words well spoken. Christian biographer Eric Metaxas wisely comments, "You can talk about right and wrong and good and bad all day long, but ultimately people need to see it. Seeing and studying the actual lives of people is simply the best way to communicate ideas about how to behave and how *not* to behave."[25] In a Christian context, godly examples provide a powerful, but often neglected, means of moral formation. Christian leaders, believing parents, and mature disciples carry a special responsibility. Will children and young believers learn what it means to live like Christ within twenty-first century culture if they do not see that life on display in mature believers? In a consumer-driven society, will they learn to practice a simple and generous lifestyle without godly examples that model that life before them? My own spiritual journey was deeply shaped by the example of my parents, whose public and private lives reflected the self-giving attitude of Jesus.

EMBODIED HOLINESS

Examples do strangely charm us into imitation. When holiness is pressed upon us we are prone to think that it is a doctrine calculated for angels and spirits whose dwelling is not with flesh. But when we read the lives of them that excelled in holiness, though they were persons of like passions with ourselves, the conviction is wonderful and powerful.[26]

—American Puritan Cotton Mather

Philosophers in Paul's world also pitted negative examples against positive ones in their moral instruction, and Paul seems to use this strategy as well. In Philippians 3, he contrasts his own Christ-oriented example (3:4–15, 17) with the bad behavior of people who should not be imitated (3:2–3, 18–19). He gives these negative examples various names, including "evil workers" (3:2) and "enemies of the cross" (3:18).

Finally, Paul offers his audience examples not only for Christlike living, but also for their participation in the mission of God. Accordingly, Paul's testimony that he continues to "preach Christ," even in the face of personal attacks (1:15–18), serves as an encouragement for the Philippians to bear costly witness in their own sphere of influence. In addition, Paul highlights the courageous witness of his fellow believers in Rome. Inspired by Paul's own faithfulness in the midst of suffering, most of these brothers and sisters "have become confident in the Lord and dare all the more to proclaim the gospel without fear" (1:14). Such fearless testimony in turn provides a positive model for the church in Philippi. It calls them, as well, to join with Paul in boldly bearing witness to the good news, even in the teeth of opposition.

To sum things up, Paul uses familiar literary and rhetorical forms from his day in the service of the gospel. He draws on the letter conventions and patterns of rhetoric of the Greco-Roman world and transforms them in a way that allows them to become instruments of forming young believers in the ways of Christ. In particular, he points them to living examples worth following, a strategy that continues to give life and breath to Christian teaching today.

SUGGESTED READING

☐ Philippians 1:3–8

☐ Philippians 3:4–19

☐ Philippians 4:9

☐ 1 Corinthians 10:31–11:1

Reflection

What are some of the cultural resources that Christians in your setting might draw from and transform in the service of Christ today?

_____

_____

_____

_____

Think of one positive example who has influenced your own Christian life. What is it about their life that helped to mentor and shape you?

_____

_____

_____

_____

_____

Who are the people whom God might want you to mentor and provide a Christian example to today?

_____

_____

_____

_____

_____

5

LIVING OUT
THE GOSPEL

How does the good news of what God has graciously done for us in Christ work out in the everyday life of God's people? This was a crucial question for Paul's audience in Philippi, and it's just as important for us today. In particular, Paul wants to show Christians what it means to live "in a manner worthy of the gospel" (Phil 1:27). He does this primarily in his exhortations to the church (1:27–2:18; 3:1–4:9). We'll explore these practical instructions over the next three chapters. First, we will consider what it means to live in faithfulness to the gospel in the face of opposition and suffering, particularly as Paul unpacks that theme in Philippians 1:27–30.

Living Out Our Citizenship

Paul launches his exhortations to the church in Philippians 1:27–30. This paragraph kicks off with a bold headline statement: "Live out your citizenship in a manner worthy of the gospel of Christ" (1:27, my translation). As Daniel Migliore wisely observes, "This is not only the first exhortation of the letter; it is a fitting summary of all the exhortations that will follow."[27] There are three things we shouldn't miss here.

First, Paul's appeal draws on *political* language. The verb in verse 27 is striking. Although it is often translated with a phrase such as "conduct yourselves" (NIV) or "live your life" (NRSV), the term literally means "live out your *citizenship*." Such language would have struck a chord with the Philippians. Residing in a Roman colony, a place where Roman laws and values carried the day, they surely understood the privileges and obligations that came with Roman citizenship. Paul says to the Philippians, in effect, "Even though you live out your citizenship—your public and common life—in a setting where Caesar claims to run the show, you must be governed by a different set of values and a higher loyalty. Your true citizenship is in heaven (3:20), not in Philippi or Rome. You worship the Lord of heaven and earth (2:10-11). So live according to the lifestyle and values of God's kingdom, not Caesar's empire."

Second, God's people are to live out this alternative life "*in a manner worthy of the gospel of Christ*" (1:27). What does a way of life that is worthy of the gospel look like? Paul unpacks what that entails in the following verses, climaxing in the story of Jesus in 2:5-11. Above all, a life worthy of the gospel is a life that's consistent with the way of Christ himself, the one who poured himself out for the sake of others, even to the point of death on a cross. Whether it's within the faith community or in the public square, we are called to reflect the gospel of Christ's self-giving love in our lifestyle and our relationships.

Third, Paul's exhortation is not only about personal behavior, but, especially, the common life of the church.

Westerners, in particular, are used to thinking in individualistic terms. We might therefore be tempted to assume that Paul is simply urging: "Each of you should live your own life in a manner worthy of the gospel."[28] But Paul's language of citizenship, as well as the thrust of the whole letter, suggest that Paul is talking primarily about how God's people live *as a community*. God has created a new humanity in Christ, which shares his life, reflects his character, and participates in his mission. As fellow citizens of the colony of Christ, we are to live out our shared life publicly. Through our loyalty to Christ and our love for others, we embody the gospel before a watching world.

This passage makes it compellingly clear that the gospel is more than a set of truths to believe or doctrines to affirm. The gospel that saves us must take on blood and bones in the lives of God's people, or it morphs into something other than the gospel. Paul surely would scratch his head at the practice of many Christian seminaries and universities to separate the study of right thinking (theology) from right living (ethics) into separate courses, or even separate departments. One of the great needs of our time is for the gospel to be preached by the common life of God's people.

A pastor friend told me about an anti-Muslim rally that was planned in his city. Social media angrily proclaimed that protesters would gather outside an Islamic mosque on a certain Friday evening to oppose and insult the worshipers as they entered the building. Protestors were encouraged to bring guns, ratcheting up the potential for violence. Hearing about this, several women from my friend's church responded, "We can't just say that we oppose this. We need to do something about it!" In response, their congregation organized a gathering of Christians from throughout their city to stand as a prayerful presence at the mosque and show that the Christian message was one of love, not hate. They met with the local imam ahead of time to discuss what they had planned. Then these Christians gathered before the protestors arrived, surrounding the entrance to the mosque. As angry protestors assembled with signs and semiautomatic weapons, shouting obscenities and burning Qur'ans, this band of Christ-followers assured their Islamic neighbors that they were welcome in their city. Some of the Christians, including teenagers, talked with the protestors, explaining that Jesus had called them to love their neighbors, not vilify them. The anger and vitriol of the situation soon diffused. Some of the protestors even seemed to experience a change of heart during the evening. The media picked up on the event, and what began as a demonstration of hatred toward Muslims transformed into a loving witness to the Islamic community and the wider public in their city. These faithful Christians not only *believed* the gospel, they *became* the gospel in the public square.

Standing Firm

The rest of chapter 1 fleshes out what it means for God's people to live out their Christian citizenship in a way that reflects the gospel of Christ. In particular, they are called to remain steadfast and united in the face of opposition and suffering. They must "stand firm," empowered by "the one Spirit" (Phil 1:27). Like athletes or soldiers uniting in a team effort, they are to strive together "for the faith of the gospel" (1:27). Most likely, this involves not only defending the truth of the gospel to unbelievers, but especially refusing to discredit the gospel through a lifestyle that is inconsistent with the good news.[29] They proclaim the gospel through both their lips and their lives.

Living in a manner worthy of the gospel also demands courage under fire. Paul urges Christ-followers not to be intimidated by those who oppose them (1:28). In a world in which virtually every public gathering became an occasion to honor the Roman emperor, Christians who opted out of such practices aroused suspicion and hostility. Paul doesn't try to water down the cost of declaring allegiance to Jesus as Lord. Is Paul concerned that the Philippians might *not* stand firm under the bombardments of their opponents? Given what he says in Philippians 1:27-30, this remains a genuine possibility.

The Gift of Suffering

For both Paul and the Philippians, living out the story of Jesus involves suffering (see 1:12, 19-20, 29-30; 2:8, 17, 29-30; 3:10; 4:11-13). One of the most jolting statements of the letter comes in Philippians 1:29: "For it has been granted to you on behalf of Christ not only to believe in him, but also to suffer for him." The verb Paul uses indicates that not only our faith, but also our *suffering* comes as a gracious gift from God. For Christians in the West, the notion of suffering as a privilege, something given to us by God, isn't an easy pill to swallow.[30] As one writer frankly observes, "We find it hard to accept that suffering happens at all, let alone that it is a gift from God."[31] What, then, are we to make of this "gift" of suffering?[32]

First, Paul isn't focusing on suffering in general, but rather suffering "on behalf of Christ" (Phil 1:29). It's the kind of suffering that happens when followers of Jesus live lives that are worthy of the gospel in a world opposed to the gospel (Phil 1:27–28). Even as Jesus suffered to the point of death on a cross (Phil 2:8), so the church must be willing to suffer for Christ's sake. Jesus himself warned his disciples that a world that was offended by him would treat his followers no differently (Matt 10:24; John 15:18–25).

This kind of suffering for Christ has been the experience of faithful Christ-followers throughout the long corridors of Christian history and remains so throughout our world today. Even as I write these words, reports of two bombings of Coptic Christian churches in Egypt, in which dozens of Palm Sunday worshipers lost their lives and scores more were injured, fill news feeds. My own understanding of Christian suffering has been profoundly shaped by humbling encounters with faithful Christians whose loyalty to Christ has cost them dearly.

One aged Chinese pastor told me the story of his experience of persecution during the early decades of communist rule in his country. He was forced to spend twenty-two years imprisoned in a labor camp, leaving his wife and six children behind. During those years, he had no Bible, no Christian community, and precious little contact with his family. He endured numbing cold, back-breaking labor, and insufficient or rancid food, and he didn't expect to survive the ordeal. At the lowest moments of his imprisonment, he would softly sing two hymns he had memorized, as an affirmation of his unswerving trust in God's grace in the midst of suffering. One was based on the words of Psalm 27: "The Lord is my light and my salvation—whom shall I fear?"; the other was a Chinese translation of "The Old Rugged Cross." Finally released, he spent another ten years confined to house arrest. Yet this undaunted servant of Christ testified with joy that he counted it a privilege to follow his Master on the way of the cross. Standing on his feet, this old pastor barely reached my shoulder; but to me he seemed like a giant in faithfulness to the gospel.

Second, the kind of suffering that Paul talks about in Philippians is a *gift* from God. Suffering in itself isn't the goal. Paul's statement has nothing to do with a twisted view of suffering that sanctions the lot of the poor, the abused, or the oppressed. We're not talking about suffering for the sake of suffering, or suffering intended to gain God's favor. While living in the Philippines, I witnessed a Good Friday procession of young men—so-called flagellantes—who beat their backs repeatedly with bamboo-tipped whips, until blood streamed down their bodies. They hoped that their self-inflicted suffering would help to purge their sins and prove their devotion to God. Such misguided action is worlds apart from Paul's meaning. Paul and the Philippians experienced suffering that originated from sinful powers opposed to the gospel, not from God. Suffering is a gracious gift, not because suffering *itself* is good, but because God can transform it into something that enables us to be conformed to the likeness of Christ.

What's more, in a world plagued by terrorism, the very attempt to connect faith with suffering and especially martyrdom causes many people to tense up. Sadly, we are all too familiar with individuals who commit horrific acts with the goal of becoming religious martyrs. But this has nothing in common with suffering and martyrdom "on behalf of Christ." Daniel Migliore puts it in no uncertain terms: "The association of what Paul says in Philippians with modern terrorist activities would be bizarre. One can hardly imagine a more egregious distortion of Paul's Letter to the Philippians than to classify it with understandings of martyrdom circulating among religious extremists today."[33] The notion of earning a heavenly reward by blowing oneself up in a crowded marketplace, trying to end as many lives as possible in the process, is the polar opposite of the gospel of Christ, the humble servant, who lovingly poured himself out for the sake of others.

What, then, does Paul's talk about the privilege of suffering for Christ have to say to Christians living in societies that are relatively free from overt persecution? I struggle with this question personally, and I don't have a fully adequate answer. But I'm convinced that, rather than either ignoring such passages or feeling guilty because they don't relate to us, we need to take them seriously. First, even if we don't face direct persecution and suffering for Christ, we can stand in solidarity with those who do. Just as Paul and the Philippians participated in a fellowship of sufferers, offering mutual support through prayer and practical aid, so we have the privilege of standing alongside of powerless and persecuted Christian communities today, upholding them by whatever means we can.

Second, *suffering* doesn't always take the form of physical deprivation or pain. Paul also testifies in Philippians, "I have suffered the loss of all things" (3:8 NRSV) for the sake of Christ. For Paul, this surely included things such as his human privileges and achievements (see 3:4-6), his status, his security, his comforts. In the case of the Philippians, loyalty to Christ no doubt cost them not only the threat of physical harm, but also the loss of social standing in a Roman colony, where being a good citizen was measured in terms of allegiance to Caesar and Rome's program of power and dominance.[34]

Surely Christian communities can increasingly expect similar kinds of loss and suffering, even in modern democratic societies, which operate under radically different notions of power, value, and status than those of the self-humbling Christ. Maybe we should ask why we don't experience more pushback than we do. Stephen Fowl observes provocatively, "The question ... becomes whether Christians in America or elsewhere testify in word and deed to a faith substantial enough to provoke opposition from powers that are either indifferent or hostile to the triune God."[35] I suspect that one reason we (myself included) find it hard to relate to the kind of Christian suffering Paul talks about in Philippians is that too often we have accommodated to the values of materialism, moral relativism, militarism, and religious pluralism, which dominate our cultural landscapes. Perhaps we would know more about the gift of suffering if we were more willing to risk "the loss of all things" for the sake of Christ.

Finally, the severe gift of suffering also becomes an opportunity to experience the irrepressible joy of Christ. In the space of one breath, Paul can testify that he is *both* suffering *and* rejoicing, along with other believers

(Phil 2:17–18). Suffering cannot rob us of our joy in Christ. Rather, it provides an opportunity for the deeply rooted joy that comes from God to reach full bloom. I witnessed a dear friend struggle for years with the ravages of amyotrophic lateral sclerosis (ALS) on his body. Yet he never ceased to exude the joy of Christ. Why? Because he maintained the joyful confidence that God was present in the midst of his suffering and that God could use even his pain and affliction to God's glory. Even in the shadowland of suffering, we have an opportunity to live "in a manner worthy of the gospel of Christ" (1:27).

SUGGESTED READING

☐ Philippians 1:19–30

☐ John 15:18–27

☐ 1 Peter 2:18–25

Reflection

Can you think of some specific ways that your Christian community might publicly embody the gospel in your world?

_____

_____

_____

_____

Is the church called to suffer for Christ in your context?
If so, in what ways? If not, why not?

_____

_____

_____

_____

What is your response to the notion of suffering as a gift of
God? Have you ever found that to be true in your own life?

_____

_____

_____

_____

6

THE MINDSET
OF JESUS

In his book *Windows of the Soul*, Ken Gire tells the story of an English missionary of a previous generation who was sent to India. His mission board insisted that he keep detailed financial records for the mission, a job for which he had no training or aptitude. He made quite a mess of the bookkeeping, until, eventually, the mission board released him. He left the mission without protest and dropped out of sight.

Years later, a female missionary arrived at a remote jungle village. She told the local people stories about Jesus from the Gospels, how he loved the poor, ate with the outcasts, fed the hungry, and visited the sick and healed them. The villagers' eyes brightened, until one of them blurted out, "We know him well; he has been living here for years!"

"When they took her to see him," Gire relates, "it was the man who years earlier had been dismissed by the mission board. ... Whenever anyone was sick, he visited them and waited up all night outside their hut, if necessary, checking on them, tending to their needs. ... For the old and the infirm, he brought food and water. When cholera broke out in the village, he went from hut to hut, doing what he could to help."[36] Although this missionary was a disaster at bookkeeping, he excelled in embodying the character of Jesus.

In this chapter, we will focus on the implications of the story of Christ in Philippians 2:1-11 for Christian living. Paul calls the church to unity through Christlike humility in 2:1-4. Then, in 2:5-11, he urges God's people to adopt the self-giving mindset of Jesus. These verses unfold a narrative that runs counter to the prevailing culture narratives not only of Paul's day, but of our own.

Be United

In one sense, Philippians 2:1-4 looks back at what Paul has just said in 1:27-30. If Christians are going to stand firm in the face of their struggle from without, they must be united within (2:1-4). At the same time, this paragraph points forward to the poem about Jesus that follows. The V-shaped story of Jesus in Phil 2:6-11 offers the supreme example of the kind of humility and self-giving love that he urges the church to live out in verses 1-4.

Philippians 2:1-4 sounds a call to unity through unselfish humility. Crucial to this appeal is Paul's desire that God's people be "like-minded" and "of one mind" (2:2). But what does this mean? Should we *always* agree with one another? Do we all need to sign up for the same detailed checklist of doctrines and behaviors?[37]

It helps to know that the word Paul uses for "mind," both here and elsewhere in Philippians (see 1:7; 3:15; 4:2, 10), represents not so much an intellectual activity as a *mindset* or life attitude, which is expressed in a certain lifestyle. Being like-minded doesn't demand that we hold identical opinions, ideas, or viewpoints. It's much more about sharing a unified purpose, embracing common priorities, adopting a shared orientation. The church isn't an army that wears the same uniform and marches in lock step. Think instead of a symphony orchestra, in which the individual members play different parts and instruments, but the result is a harmonious symphony.

Being united involves "having the same love" for one another (2:2). This is a love that has its source in Christ (2:1) and becomes visible in his self-emptying service to others (2:6–8). Unity also means subordinating our rights and preferences for the sake of others in Christian humility (2:3–4). In the Philippians' world, humility never would have made a top-ten list of virtues. On the contrary, people generally peered down their noses at humility as the degrading, groveling attitude of a slave. But for Paul, the church's humility is shaped not by cultural values, but by Jesus himself, a Master who embraced a slave's role and washed his disciples' filthy feet (John 13:1–17). In Philippians 2, Paul's call to treat others with humility points forward to the story of Christ that follows. There Paul describes Jesus as the one who "humbled himself by becoming obedient to death ... on a cross" (Phil 2:8). Jesus' own life and death transforms humility from forced self-abasement to a freely chosen, loving service to others, in conformity with the mindset of Christ.

Paul's message to the church in Phil 2:1–4 is clear: without humility, there's no true unity. He urges, "Value others above yourselves, not looking to your own interests but each of you to the interests of the others" (2:3–4). This has nothing to do with either false modesty or an inferiority complex. Rather, Paul calls the entire church to prioritize the needs and concerns of others, instead of viewing life through the filter of their own self-interest.

Paul's emphasis on Christian unity in Philippians isn't merely a theoretical discussion. Later in the letter, Paul pleads with two church leaders, named Euodia and Syntyche, to "be of the same mind in the Lord" (4:2).

DIETRICH BONHOEFFER'S TAKE ON CHRISTIAN UNITY

During the gathering storm of Nazism in Germany, theologian Dietrich Bonhoeffer established an under-the-radar seminary to train pastors in 1935. In the two years before the Gestapo closed the seminary down, Bonhoeffer and the students under his care tried to live out Scripture's call to Christian unity in their everyday relationships. Bonhoeffer reflects on the basis of Christian community in his classic book, *Life Together*:

> Our community with one another consists solely in what Christ has done to both of us. … I have community with others and I shall continue to have it only through Jesus Christ. The more genuine and the deeper our community becomes, the more will everything else between us recede, the more clearly and purely will Jesus Christ and his work become the one and only thing that is vital between us. We have one another only through Christ, but through Christ we do have one another, wholly, and for all eternity.[39]

Paul includes these women among his leadership team, his coworkers, who have participated in his gospel ministry (4:3).[38] He doesn't tell us the specific nature of the differences between them. But that Paul spotlights their disagreement in this way suggests both that it was public knowledge and that it threatened to poison the unity of the church. For Paul, the stakes are far too high simply to ignore the problem. He calls both parties to be reconciled by laying aside their differences and adopting a common mindset (Phil 4:2). Once again, the church's unity is rooted in the willingness of God's people to embrace the mindset of Christ himself, the one who humbled himself for the sake of others, even to the point of laying down his life for them (2:5-11).

Unity, Not Uniformity

Christian unity, then, emerges as one of the key themes in Philippians (see 1:27; 2:1-4; 3:15; 4:2-3). For Paul, the oneness of the church is fundamental to *who we are* as God's people. It's part of what it means to live out the story of Jesus in our everyday relationships, as we show others a Jesus-style love that puts their interests ahead of our own (2:1-5). That's not to say we have to become Christian clones who all speak, think, and act the same. We don't get to choose the members of the family of God any more than we can choose the members of our biological families. Our unity is not based on our attending the same church, sharing the same political perspective, or going through the same discipleship training. We are one because we are united with the same Lord. That supreme relationship makes all the difference.

I have spent most of my ministry in theological institutions in Asia and Europe in which students hailed from an artist's palette of countries and cultures. Some of those cultures represented historic enemies who had waged wars against one another. I sat across the dinner table from a Korean student who confessed, "I was brought up to hate the Japanese people for what they did to us during World War II. When I came here to study, I was very prejudiced against them. But I've been watching the lives of the Japanese students, and I've seen they love God deeply and are some of the best Christians I know. God has changed my attitude. Now I see them as brothers and sisters in Christ." In a world that divides people, splinters communities, and pits one group against another, such unnatural oneness becomes a compelling witness to the reconciling work of Christ. In another letter, Paul assures us that Christ himself "is our peace, who has made the two groups one and has destroyed the barrier, the dividing wall of hostility" (Eph 2:14).

Dealing with Disagreements

At the same time, Paul does not simply take a "live and let live" approach to all matters of Christian belief and practice. In Philippians 3:15–16, he addresses the thorny issue of Christians who disagree with one another: "All of us ... who are mature should take such a view of things. And if on some point you think differently, that too God will make clear to you. Only let us live up to what we have already attained." Paul is realistic enough to recognize that not all believers are spiritually mature and that some attitudes need to change.

How do Paul's instructions to the Philippians speak to churches that must deal with divergent attitudes today?[40] First, Paul models remarkable patience toward those who think differently. He trusts the Holy Spirit to faithfully correct the people of God. Like Paul, when no life-or-death issue is at stake, we need to give time for the Spirit to do his work in their hearts and minds. We can exhort, encourage, preach, teach, remind, and reprimand. But ultimately, it is *God* who will transform people's attitudes.

Second, whatever our disagreements on specific issues, the church needs to focus on what is essential (3:16)—our common loyalty to Christ and the loving, cross-shaped life that entails. We are continually called back to our defining story, the story of Jesus sent, crucified, risen, and reigning as Lord. It is this old, gospel story, the story that Christians have embraced and sometimes died for throughout the centuries, that we must embody in our world (1:27). We cannot allow ourselves to become divided over lesser things.

Third, it follows that Christian leaders and communities need to take care regarding what they treat as being essential and how much they insist on correcting other believers. I have witnessed missionaries from the West trying to impose their own "authorized version" of Christian doctrine and practice on believers in other world areas—a particular understanding of the end times, for example, or certain cultural notions of how Christians ought to conduct themselves in church. Yes, there are borders that shouldn't be crossed, but we need to make sure that those boundaries come from the *gospel* and not our own preferences.

Fourth, Paul doesn't spell out in detail how much divergence in belief and practice is acceptable within the Christian community. This is a tough question, especially in light of the increasing polarization that seems to plague much contemporary thinking, on the one hand, and the plea for a tolerance that will accept virtually *anything*, on the other. Navigating these choppy waters is the hard work of the whole Christian community, in all of its various global manifestations, and not simply that of individual believers. At the end of the day, "our efforts to discern the limits of Christian difference must be rooted in Scripture, guided by the Spirit, informed by the historic and intercultural understanding of the church, and in line with the transforming mission of God in the world."[41]

Adopt the Mindset of Jesus

Earlier we saw that the V-shaped story of Jesus' humbling himself and being exalted (Phil 2:6–11) forms the theological heart of the letter. In one sense, everything that Paul writes in Philippians before this passage points toward the story of Jesus, and much of what follows lies in its shadow. We need to be clear, however, about Paul's reason for including this narrative of Jesus' history in the letter. Paul introduces the passage with a headline imperative: "Have this mindset among yourselves, which was also in Christ Jesus" (2:5, my translation). Immediately before Paul narrates how Jesus emptied himself and humbled himself even to the point of dying on a cross, he says to the Christian community, "In your thinking and acting, follow Christ Jesus."[42] Then and now, this narrative of self-giving love is not just the story of Jesus; it is also the story of the church.

Here are two further points we shouldn't miss. First, this call to have the mindset of Christ is not simply about the attitude of each individual believer, but applies to the whole Christian community ("among yourselves," 2:5). The story of Christ needs to shape how Christians relate to one another. Second, this cross-shaped way of thinking and living isn't limited to relationships among Christians. Only if God's people embody Jesus' self-giving love for others will they be able to live in a manner worthy of the gospel in the public square, particularly among those who oppose them (1:27–28). If the gospel is a story of self-giving love, then that story must be lived out both inside and outside the church.

Paul's primary aim, then, in relating the story of Jesus in Philippians 2 is not to tell Christians *what* to believe *about* Christ, but rather *how* to live *like* Christ. Conformity to the pattern of Jesus, particularly his self-giving death on the cross, is basic to Paul's understanding of the Christian life (see, e.g., Rom 8:17, 29; Gal 2:19–20). In Eugene Peterson's language, instead of listing a set of rules and urging us, "Live up to this," Paul tells the story of Jesus and says, "Live *into* this."[43] This comprises Paul's crucial strategy for moral formation in Philippians. He not only directly urges us to live in ways that are worthy of the gospel (Phil 1:27–2:4). He also points us to the story of Jesus, which forms the heart of the gospel, as the basis and reason for doing so. Like Jesus, like Christians. The story of Jesus is *our* story, as well. We are called to reenact the Jesus-drama every day on the streets of our cities and in the webs of our relationships.

Moving On Down

What does this look like, practically?[44] Some Christians have tried to imitate Jesus' actions in a highly literal way. Think, for example, of St. Francis and his followers in the Middle Ages, who sought to emulate Jesus' wandering life of poverty. Or the Filipino Christians who on Good Friday go to the point of having themselves nailed to an actual cross. Living out the story of Jesus, however, doesn't require us to mimic his specific actions, especially if we try to do so through human efforts.

How, then, does Jesus serve as a pattern for our lives today? First, the focus in Philippians falls on embracing the *mindset* of Jesus. We don't have to copy all of the details of Jesus' earthly life. But we *are* called to conform to his life attitude of humility, obedience, and self-giving love, both as individuals and as Christian communities. In other words, we must find appropriate, context-specific ways to live out the Jesus-story in our own neighborhoods and workplaces.

Second, this isn't something we can do in our own strength. It is only the transforming work of Christ within us and the empowering of his Spirit that make it possible for us to retell the story of Jesus through our lives and our loving relationships. Only because Jesus took the downward path to the cross (2:8) and because he reigns as living Lord (2:11) are we able to live as obedient communities, reflecting his own character.

In the end, what the Christ poem calls us to is less about *imitating* Christ than it is about *being conformed to his likeness*—through the power of the Holy Spirit within us. Dallas Willard puts it well: "Jesus calls us to him to impart himself to us. He does not call us to do what he did, but to be who he was, permeated with love. Then the doing of what he said and did becomes the natural expression of who we are in him."[45] At its core, Christian holiness is about *Christlikeness*. Living out the story of Jesus means allowing Christ to live out his life of self-emptying love through us, both inside and outside the church.

Who comes to *your* mind when you think of a life of humble, self-giving love? My thoughts turn to my dad. My father retired early from his leadership role in his denomination so that he and my mother could begin speaking in various church services and mission conferences. Because of my mother's involvement in a mission organization, this involved traveling internationally and speaking. My parents were thrilled with the opportunities for ministry that God had opened up for them. They eagerly anticipated the future. But then my mother was afflicted with Alzheimer's disease. Suddenly, everything changed. They had to cancel all of their speaking engagements, and for the next seven years, my father spent virtually all of his time caring for my mother. The more the disease progressed, the more difficult and degrading that service became. I can picture him sitting next to my mother on their bed, feeding her a spoonful of food at a time, like one would an infant. I never heard him complain.

One day, after my mother's death, I asked him about it. "Dad," I said, "that must have been so hard!" He answered,

"When I had to give up preaching and any kind of public ministry, I felt so useless to God. One day, I was talking to God about this and feeling very sorry for myself. But the Lord seemed to say to me, 'Floyd, *this* is your ministry.' And I realized that caring for my wife in her time of need was just as important as anything else I had done in Christian service. From that point on, I saw my taking care of your mother as my very best service to Christ."

Competing Stories

I noted earlier that the story of Jesus' self-giving love clashed with the prevailing narratives of the Roman world. These were stories that promised peace and security through the iron fist of imperial power, stories that pictured life as a contest, in which you competed with others as you tried to move up the ladder of status and honor. In that kind of world, the story of Jesus choosing the way of *downward* mobility and lowly service didn't make any sense.

But is it different today? Taking the *lower* place, putting the needs of others first isn't normal in *our* world, either. We hear stories that tell us that the great goal in life is to achieve financial success and the influence that follows. In the West, popular culture beckons us to put our individual rights, security, and happiness ahead of what might benefit others, especially those who are different than we are. We're even tempted to view Christian faith as a means to attaining personal fulfillment and happiness, rather than as a path to serving Christ and others. In my own case, I can easily begin to see myself in competition with other ministers and educators for recognition, approval, and success.

Resisting the competing cultural stories isn't easy. Downward social mobility is no more popular in the twenty-first century than it was in the first century. But the people of God must live into a different story, a story whose symbols are the towel and the cross, a story of self-emptying love. As Jesus put it, "Whoever wants to be my disciple must deny themselves and take up their cross daily and follow me" (Luke 9:23).

SUGGESTED READING

☐ Philippians 2:1–11

☐ Philippians 3:15–16

☐ Philippians 4:2–3

☐ John 13:34–35

☐ John 17:20–26

Reflection

Suppose that two groups of Christians in your local church strongly disagree over a nonessential issue. In light of the teaching in Philippians, what practical steps would you suggest taking to deal with the disagreement?

_____

_____

_____

_____

What is one practical way in which God might enable you or your Christian community to reenact the Jesus-drama of Philippians 2:6–11 in everyday life?

_____

_____

_____

_____

How does the story of Jesus' self-giving love collide with the common stories of your culture? Identify one or two stories that are incompatible with the story of Christ in Philippians 2.

_____

_____

_____

_____

7

A MISSIONAL COMMUNITY

It was early morning. I sat in a bakery, sharing a breakfast of bagels and coffee with a friend, the pastor of a local congregation in a rather depressed area of the city. We began to talk about what it means to do evangelism in North America today. His next statement (which I'll paraphrase) caught me off guard.

> I do my best to represent Christ to the people who live in my neighborhood. I've tried to get to know them and befriend them. I shovel snow from the driveways of elderly people in the winter. I do odd jobs for neighbors who need help. When they face trouble with sickness or tense relationships with their kids, I try to be present and listen to their concerns. I do my best to love them as Jesus would. But I don't talk about my faith. People have heard too many words. They don't want more words from Christians. I'm trying to live the good news before them.[46]

Was my friend right? Is it enough simply to let our lives do the talking? Or is a verbal testimony always needed for the gospel to be communicated? Paul's Letter to the Philippians speaks to the character of our Christian witness. The story of Jesus in chapter two carries implications not only for how we relate to one another as Christians, but also for how we live out the mission of God in our world.

Work Out Your Salvation

Paul immediately follows up the story of Jesus, humbled and exalted, in Philippians 2:6–11 by applying it to the concrete realities of the church in 2:12–18. He urges the Philippians: "continue to work out your salvation with fear and trembling" (2:12). What is *that* about? Clearly, working *out* our salvation is not the same as working *for* our salvation. Paul consistently teaches that people are saved by the grace of God and not by human effort (e.g., Rom 4:5; Eph 2:8). He has already assured the Philippians that their salvation originates from God (Phil 1:28; see also 3:9). And in Philippians 2:13, he reminds the church that it is God who works in them, enabling them to will and to act according to his saving purpose. We can only *work out* what God has already *worked in*.

What's more, Paul's appeal involves more than how individual Christians experience personal salvation, although that is surely assumed. In particular, Paul is concerned with how God's gift of salvation is lived out in the context of the Christian community. Working out our salvation, then, involves our intentional response to what God has graciously done for us in Christ. This entails a life of daily, disciplined obedience as we cooperate in God's transforming work within us, both as individuals and as a body of believers. If we want to spy some snapshots of what actively living out our salvation looks like, the surrounding verses provide plenty of material. Among other things, it means:

- working together as a unified people with a common mindset (Phil 2:1–4)

- allowing God to conform us to a lifestyle of humility and self-giving love toward others (2:5–11)

- putting a stop to internal bickering and living as a holy and missional people within a crooked world (2:14–16)

What's more, this *salvation* leans into the future. God has promised that he will complete the saving work he began within and among us (1:6). He invites us, however, to wholeheartedly and obediently live out that salvation now, in light of God's ultimate restoring purpose for the whole world.

But why does Paul say that we should do this with "fear and trembling" (2:12)? Here he appeals to Old Testament language (see, e.g., Deut 2:25). The point is not that we should cower before God because he is out to get us. Rather, "fear and trembling" signals an attitude of awe and reverence, entirely appropriate for people who live out their salvation in the presence of the living God. It reminds us that the Christian response to God's grace is never casual or complacent. The life of obedience takes full intentionality and determined effort.[47]

Be Partners in the Gospel

The Grace of Giving

In Philippians, living in a manner that is worthy of the gospel (Phil 1:27) involves participating in God's mission. From the church's beginning days, the Philippians have shared in a "partnership in the gospel" with Paul (1:5). What shape does this gospel partnership take? For one thing, this local congregation participates in Paul's gospel ministry, both by interceding for Paul in prayer (1:19) and through their generosity (4:14–15). The latter includes gifts of money (4:10–20), as well as sending coworkers such as Epaphroditus to give Paul practical help (2:25–30).

It's noteworthy that Paul's willingness to receive financial gifts from the Philippians bucks his normal practice. In the case of the church in Corinth, for example, Paul expresses concern that accepting money might hinder the progress of the gospel (1 Cor 9:18). Such a deterrent might come if the Corinthians, or at least a group of them, claimed Paul as a client who was continually obligated to them, due to their financial support. Gifts that came with strings attached might hinder Paul's ability to preach the gospel freely (1 Cor 9:18). But Paul apparently held no such qualms regarding the Philippians. Instead, he views their relationship as a mutual partnership of equals in the service of the gospel (Phil 4:15). "Paul considers the Philippians' financial support as a full partnership in the mission of God, not a second-rate contribution."[48]

Radical generosity still serves as a telling barometer of our faithfulness to God and God's mission in the world. Giving to God and others is no less "spiritual" a practice than attending church or reading the Bible. If God owns our wallets, our checkbooks, and our credit cards, he has *us*. Ultimately, what Paul calls the "grace of giving" (2 Cor 8:7) is as important for the givers as it is for those who receive the gift. It demonstrates God's grace at work in and through our lives (see Phil 4:17).

This matter of "giving and receiving" (Phil 4:15) carries a special challenge for Christian communities in the affluent societies of our world. What does it mean to practice a partnership of giving and receiving with the global family of God, in a world where the chasm between the haves and the have-nots continually expands? There's no single answer. But surely those of us who are relatively blessed materially need to ask God to convict and enable us to cheerfully give more of those resources away.

Embodying the Good News

The Philippians' gospel partnership takes another form in this letter. Christians actively share in the advance of the good news where they are, both through their words and their lives. Paul spotlights the congregation's witness to those outside the fellowship in Philippians 2:14-16. On the negative side, God's people must avoid complaining and arguing (2:14). Such internal bickering could easily snuff out the flame of the church's witness before a watching world. Positively, they must live as God's holy people, above reproach, in the midst of a twisted and corrupt environment (2:15). On the one hand, their distinctive, holy lives will display a visible difference to the surrounding culture. On the other, the church's integrity and unity will shine like stars in the night sky. Such a beacon of authenticity will attract others to their Lord, like moths drawn to a flame. In other words, a church that embodies the good news of Christ will carry a transforming influence in its world.

Making this practical, Christian husbands and wives can model servanthood and faithfulness in societies where family relationships too often exhibit selfishness, abuse, and disposable relationships. Likewise, when Christian leaders show integrity in their speech, their finances, and their sexuality, when they are more concerned with serving others than promoting themselves, they project a striking alternative to many of the power brokers in their culture. Whenever the church lives as a winsome, contrast community, others can't help but notice. And some will be attracted by the difference.

At the same time, Paul urges the church to "hold out the word of life" to others (Phil 2:16, my translation). The verb Paul uses here could mean "hold *on to* the word of life"; that is, hold steady in your faith. Or, it could signify, "hold *forth* the word of life," which implies sharing the good news with others. I lean toward the latter translation.[50] But even if Paul is calling the church to hold fast *to* the gospel, this still implies active mission. If God's people remain faithful to the gospel, that surely includes sharing the good news—the word that imparts life—when they have the opportunity. As Michael Gorman asks, can we imagine believers in Philippi living a countercultural lifestyle, regularly worshiping Jesus as Lord rather than Caesar, without ever being asked to explain their strange behavior or having the occasion to introduce their friends to the story of Jesus?[51] That's unlikely.

A true "partnership in the gospel" (1:5), then, engages both the words we speak and the lives we live. Consequently, when Paul urges, "Let your gentleness be evident to all" (4:5), I suspect he has in mind both gentle speech and a gentle spirit, which allow our unbelieving neighbors to catch a glimpse of Jesus. Ultimately, mission is not simply about what we as God's people *do* or *say*. It is who we *are*.

COFFEE SHOP MISSION

I watched my father, in his later years, embody the mission of God in his public world. After he retired from many years of leadership ministry in the church, a local coffee shop became his mission field. My father made it his destination every morning, and, over time, he became enmeshed in the lives of the regular patrons and employees. I watched him call them by name, ask them about their families and their health concerns, and listen to their hopes, their longings, their fears. He prayed for some of them by name every day. And, when the Spirit prompted, he spoke to them of a God who loves, forgives, and reconciles.

When my father was afflicted with an aggressive brain tumor, his final outing was to visit his friends at the coffee shop. Arriving in his wheelchair, he was greeted by about fifteen patrons, who had gathered to express their farewells. Many of them made a point to tell me how his joyful, loving spirit had touched their lives, how much they would miss him. My father sought out a young man among the group, who, through his influence, had come to believe in Jesus as Lord. "I'm passing the torch on to you," my father told him. "Now this is *your* mission field."[49]

Focus on Virtue

How should God's people relate to the culture around them? Our study of Philippians makes clear that for God's people, faithfulness to the gospel involves embracing a higher allegiance and a different set of priorities from the prevailing culture. What's more, Paul's audience is well acquainted with the sting of hostility from the society in which they live. Does this mean that Christians should reject everything about the surrounding culture? Not at all. Paul speaks to this issue near the end of his final exhortations to the church (4:2–9). He urges: "Finally, brothers and sisters, whatever is true, whatever is noble, whatever is right, whatever is pure, whatever is lovely, whatever is admirable—if anything is excellent or praiseworthy—think about such things" (4:8).

In this text, Paul seems to go out of his way to choose terms that would have rung a bell for readers in the Roman world. Such virtues were promoted by pagan moral teachers and widely valued in the Greco-Roman culture of the time. This raises a question, however. We've seen that Paul says a great deal in this letter that challenges Roman cultural values. Why, then, does he suddenly seem to endorse the moral ideals of the prevailing culture?

Three considerations help us to see that Paul does not give blanket approval to Roman cultural values.[52] First, these virtues are not the *exclusive* property of the pagans. Nearly all of these terms also appear in the Greek translation of the Old Testament.

Second, Paul does not encourage his audience to embrace *everything* in Greco-Roman morality. Rather, he only points to "what he considers the *highest* and the *best* in pagan thought and culture."[53]

Third, Paul doesn't intend for the Philippians to understand what is noble or excellent in precisely the same way the Romans do. If we continue reading, we discover that Paul interprets verse 8 with the challenge that follows in Philippians 4:9. There Paul urges his readers to learn from his example, even as he embodies the self-giving pattern of Jesus Christ. This surely implies that the values Christians share with the wider culture *are always transformed in some way* by the gospel. For God's people, they are only *Christian* virtues when they are lived out in light of the gospel. But that should come as no surprise. All of Paul's exhortations in Philippians arc back to what it means to live in a way that is worthy of the gospel (1:27), a gospel that is defined by Jesus' story of self-giving love (2:6–11).

Philippians 4:8 affords us a valuable perspective as we engage our cultural worlds today. On the one hand, we are free to celebrate what is true and good and lovely in our cultures. We can recognize such things as expressions of God's many-colored grace at work in the world. We don't have to pooh-pooh everything outside the church as inferior or even hostile to the kingdom of God. Consequently, we are free to enjoy the beauty of the artistic and literary expressions of our cultures and learn from them. Likewise, we can join hands with people of various persuasions in promoting justice for the poor and the marginalized or in caring for a beleaguered creation.

At the same time, Philippians 4:9 reminds us that we cannot embrace the values and expressions of our cultures uncritically. Guided by the Spirit, there are times to say "no" or "yes, but" to popular values in our culture. For example, some common understandings of truth in my own North American culture can't be reconciled with the gospel. A Christ-shaped notion of truth challenges widely accepted claims that all truth is relative or that it can be known only through personal experience. Our understanding of what is true cannot bow down to the idol of "tolerance," which bans us from questioning anyone's personal conduct, even when it involves lying to an employer or cheating on a spouse.[54] The well-worn mantra "Nobody's perfect!" doesn't excuse bad behavior.

The ultimate test of what is true and good in the art forms or values of our cultures is whether they are compatible with the cross-shaped story of Christ. By critically engaging our cultures, God's people can shine forth as a beacon of light in the midst of a dark, desperate world.

Do you remember the story that started this chapter? Although I have much sympathy with my friend's concern that the gospel be lived out in his neighborhood, I can't agree that words aren't called for. We learn from Philippians that living out the story of Jesus involves a show-and-tell witness. Paul would surely say that we not only need to embody the gospel with our lives, but, at some point, we also need to tell the story with our lips. This marriage of telling, doing, and being the good news enables Christian communities today to *become* the mission of God in their world.

SUGGESTED READING

☐ Philippians 2:12–18

☐ Philippians 4:4–20

☐ 2 Corinthians 8:1–15

☐ Colossians 4:5–6

☐ 1 Peter 3:13–16

Reflection

What is your response to the statement, "If God owns our wallets, our checkbooks, and our credit cards, he has *us*"? Do you have any fears or hesitations about getting more involved in Christian giving? If so, what are they?

_____

_____

_____

Write down some specific arenas of life in which your actions and attitudes or those of your Christian community might make the good news attractive to outsiders today.

_____

_____

_____

Can you think of some widely held values of your own culture that are compatible with the gospel of Christ crucified? What about specific cultural values that the gospel calls into question?

_____

_____

_____

8

CONCLUSION

Philippians is a story-shaped letter. It's as if the Philippians ask Paul, "Tell us a story!" and Paul shares a narrative that is far more beautiful and profound than they ever could have imagined. This story—the story of stories, the story of what God has done in his Son to redeem people and restore all things—touches every nook and cranny of Philippians. Paul tells that story explicitly in Philippians 2:6–11. But it plays out elsewhere in a variety of ways, like variations on the main theme of an orchestral symphony. To wrap up this book, I'd like to summarize some key aspects of that story we have discovered along the way.

A Good-News Story

The V-shaped story that Paul narrates in Philippians 2:6–11 is embedded at the heart of the gospel that Paul proclaims and lives out. It's the story of Jesus' descent from the heights of glory to the depths of human vulnerability and suffering, even to the extreme act of self-giving love—death on a cross. But it is also the story of victory over the grave and God exalting Jesus as living and reigning Lord, before whom the entire cosmos will bow in the end. When we ask the question, "What is the gospel?" this is where we need to begin. The good news is bigger than many of us have imagined.

It embraces not simply God's desire to save people from their sins, but also God's ultimate purpose to reconcile to himself *all* things in heaven and on earth in Christ (Col 1:20; see Rom 8:18–25; Eph 1:9–10). Philippians 2:9–11 announces that what God is up to in the world won't reach its goal until every part of creation acknowledges Jesus' lordship and gives glory to God. Any understanding we might offer of "how to get saved" or "how to get to heaven" must flow out of this story of God's loving action in Jesus' life, death, resurrection, and glorious return, or it is merely a half-baked gospel. Philippians makes clear that the gospel is anchored not in what happens *to* us, but what God has done *for* us and the whole world in Christ.

A Lived-Out Story

Philippians 2:5 only makes obvious what Paul tells us in various ways throughout the letter: the story of Jesus' self-giving love is *our* story, as well. We are to "have the same mindset as Christ Jesus." As individuals and as God's community, we are to live in a way that's worthy of the gospel (1:27). As I said near the beginning of this book, the V-shaped story of Jesus represents *both* the source of our salvation *and* the pattern of our lives.

This means that any attempts to separate beliefs and behavior are, in the end, quite misguided. If you and I don't allow the gospel that saved us to become visibly evident in how we handle adversity or in the way we treat others, we effectively deny the truth of the good news. If our story carries any hope of addressing an increasingly skeptical world, it must, by the power of the Spirit, be authentically embodied in the lives of God's people. There is nothing more compelling than a Christian community that looks like Jesus.

A Cross-Shaped Story

The story we are drawn into comes in the shape of a cross. Philippians shines a spotlight on the downward movement of the Jesus way. Christ makes himself nothing, humbles himself, and willingly hangs spread-eagle on a cross—all for the sake of others. This story of radical servant-love not only shows us what God is like, but it also calls God's people into a life that's conformed to (Christ's) death (Phil 3:10). Paul peppers this letter with examples of what that looks like in flesh and bone, including his own story. Our challenge today is to live into that story in our everyday lives—to allow God to transform us into the likeness of Christ and his cross.

Philippians doesn't picture the Christian life as a holiday cruise on smooth waters. Knowing Christ deeply draws us into *both* his resurrection power *and* the fellowship of his sufferings (3:10). Philippians leaves no room for wimpy discipleship. It beckons us to jump into the deep end of the pool. It invites us to embrace a Christ-enabled contentment that will sustain us in the triumphs and tragedies of our lives (4:11–13).

A Common-Life Story

Philippians forcefully reminds us that living out the Jesus story is no solo performance. We act out this drama as part of a closely knit cast of fellow players. Having the mindset of Jesus means treating others in the community with the same servant-love that we see in Jesus. This letter places a high premium on the unity of Christ's body. Divisions and power games within the Christian community can frustrate the body's ability to function, not to mention quenching the flame of Christian witness. In a world of fractured relationships, global conflicts, polarized ideologies, and self-promoting ambitions, the love and unity of a church stands as a powerful and persuasive embodiment of the gospel.

An Others-Oriented Story

Christian communities reenact the Jesus drama in the midst of a "warped and crooked" world (2:15). Jesus' example of cross-shaped love becomes the pattern of our relationships with others, both inside and outside the church. Philippians calls us into a missional partnership of prayer, generosity, service, proclamation, and suffering. If we take the message of Philippians seriously, mission will become more than a strategy and a program. It will define who we are, as the people of God.

A Joy-Filled Story

Philippians bubbles with the joy of Christ. From start to finish, joy remains the atmosphere in which the entire letter breathes. Repeatedly, Paul bears witness to his own joy and urges others to rejoice with him. This is all the more stunning given that in Philippians, joy emerges out of the crucible of hardship and suffering (1:18; 2:17–18,

28–29). This Philippians kind of joy means far more than a feeling of happiness or a positive attitude that we dredge up from within. It is joy "in Christ Jesus" (3:3), anchored in the rock-solid confidence that God is working in and among us, accomplishing our salvation, conforming us to the loving pattern of Jesus, and using even our most desperate circumstances to the glory of God (1:12). Whatever else might be said about the Christian life, it is a story of joy in Christ. A Christian without joy makes about as much sense as an ocean without water.[55]

This isn't just a pleasant platitude. I am finishing this book in the midst of the global COVID-19 crisis. Each day brings news of inconceivable suffering, hardship, and fear, particularly among the most vulnerable in our world. As someone in a higher-risk population group, I live out my days in isolation from family and friends, and like the incarcerated Paul, I'm uncertain of what the future holds. At times, I feel overwhelmed. Is it possible to experience true joy in the midst of a time like this? Yes. It is. God is teaching me to draw from his deep reservoir of joy, a joy that focuses on the faithfulness of God and not on the fear of the moment. I am learning to affirm with Paul, "But even if ... I am glad and rejoice with all of you" (2:17).

Philippians' sonata of joy reaches a crescendo in Paul's ringing call to the church in 4:4: "Rejoice in the Lord *always*. I will say it again: Rejoice!" Daniel Migliore reflects on this remarkable summons: "Paul's urging here is probably best rendered not in words alone but in words accompanied by soaring music: Handel's 'Hallelujah Chorus,' or the lines of the familiar hymn set to the final movement of Beethoven's Ninth Symphony: 'Joyful, joyful, we adore Thee, God of glory, Lord of love.' "[56] Indeed, joy and deep gratitude are the only fitting responses to the magnificent story of God's loving, redeeming mission in Christ that Philippians tells, a story that transforms us into his image, a story that is retold again and again in the chapters that make up our daily lives and relationships. "Rejoice in the Lord always" (Phil 4:4). How could we respond otherwise?

A Personal Postscript

Let me close with a personal story. Near the end of Philippians, prisoner Paul graces the Philippians—and us—with a magnificent promise: "And my God will fully supply all your needs according to his riches in glory in Christ Jesus" (Phil 4:19, my translation). Earlier in my life, I sensed that God was leading me into further studies, in preparation for teaching the Bible in a global setting. After much prayer, I developed a growing conviction that I should study at a university in Scotland. But I confronted a massive obstacle: I didn't have the funds to finance that education. Not even close! I searched diligently (without the help of the web!) for any form of scholarship or grant that might help fund my education. Every inquiry led to a dead end. I had no option but to release the matter to God and trust that if this was his leading, he would somehow provide a way. During that period of waiting, Philippians 4:19 became an anchor for me. It helped me trust that God would fully supply.

In time, God graciously began to work in some astounding ways. He provided an unexpected grant for my tuition, and even support for my living expenses, through a generous Christian family. I was able to piece together the needed funding for my studies. The need was *fully supplied*.

But the story doesn't end there. During my period of study in a new country, I encountered loneliness, discouragement, lack of success in my studies, and an extended physical illness, which doctors couldn't identify. I was ready to give up and go home. Why had God led me into an ordeal that seemed destined to end in failure? It didn't make sense. In the midst of my wilderness of discouragement, I sensed the Spirit drawing me once again to Philippians 4:19. I came to realize that God's promise applied to far more than finances. Could I trust God to fully supply *all* my needs? As I began to release my personal struggles, my health, my studies—everything—to God, his limitless resources in Christ proved altogether sufficient. I learned that my God was more than capable of providing what I lacked in every arena of life. It's a lesson I am still learning, even now.

As we conclude this study of Philippians, my prayer for you is that you may increasingly know this God whose story of amazing, self-giving love in Christ the letter tells. May you experience his unfaltering faithfulness to provide *all* your needs in Christ Jesus. "To our God and Father be glory for ever and ever. Amen" (Phil 4:20).

Reflection

Which aspect of the story Philippians tells discussed in this conclusion speaks most into your journey with Christ right now? Why?

_____

_____

_____

_____

List three takeaways from your study of Philippians that you think are important to remember and apply.

_____

_____

_____

_____

In what areas of your life do you need God to fully supply all your need through his riches in Christ today (Phil 4:19)?

_____

_____

_____

_____

RECOMMENDED READING

Read and reread Philippians, preferably in different translations. There is no substitute for saturating ourselves in the text of Scripture. For more in-depth study in Philippians, here are several commentary resources to explore:

- Markus Bockmuehl, *The Epistle to the Philippians*, Black's New Testament Commentary (repr., Grand Rapids: Baker Academic, 2013). A highly readable, midsize commentary, rich with insight into the text.

- Lynn H. Cohick, *Philippians*, The Story of God Bible Commentary (Grand Rapids: Zondervan, 2013). A well-written and highly accessible commentary that is especially strong on application.

- Dean Flemming, *Philippians: A Commentary in the Wesleyan Tradition*, New Beacon Bible Commentary (Kansas City, MO: Beacon Hill, 2009). My commentary looks at each section of Philippians in light of its background, its theological message, and its significance for Christians today.

- Daniel L. Migliore, *Philippians and Philemon*,
  Belief: A Theological Commentary on the Bible
  (Louisville: Westminster John Knox, 2014).
  A solid theological interpretation of Philippians
  and Philemon.

NOTES

1. N. T. Wright, "Book of Philippians," in *Dictionary of Theological Interpretation of the Bible*, ed. Kevin J. Vanhoozer (Grand Rapids: Baker, 2005), 588.

2. This outline is adapted from Dean Flemming, *Philippians: A Commentary in the Wesleyan Tradition*, New Beacon Bible Commentary (Kansas City, MO: Beacon Hill, 2009), 5–6.

3. Flemming, *Philippians*, 28.

4. See Flemming, *Philippians*, 40.

5. Morna D. Hooker, "The Letter to the Philippians," in *The New Interpreter's Bible* (Nashville: Abingdon, 2000), 11:476.

6. See Joseph H. Hellerman, *Reconstructing Honor in Roman Philippi: Carmen Christi as Crucis Pudorum*, Society for New Testament Studies Monograph Series 132 (Cambridge: Cambridge University Press, 2005), 146–47.

7. The following paragraphs adapt some material from Flemming, *Philippians*, 123–24.

8. Flemming, *Philippians*, 119.

9. Karl Barth, *The Epistle to the Philippians*, trans. J. W. Leitch (London: SCM, 1962), 66.

10. Augustine, *Sermon* 207; cited in Michael J. Gorman, *Apostle of the Crucified Lord: A Theological Introduction to Paul and His Letters* (Grand Rapids: Eerdmans, 2004), 450.

11. The following paragraphs adapt some material from Flemming, *Philippians*, 173–75.

12. Lynn H. Cohick, *Philippians*, The Story of God Bible Commentary (Grand Rapids: Zondervan, 2013), 171.

13. See Fred Craddock, *Philippians*, Interpretation (John Knox: Atlanta, 1985), 61.

14. Melba Padilla Maggay, *The Gospel In Filipino Context* (Manila: OMF Literature, 1987), 8.

15. Flemming, *Philippians*, 180.

16. See Flemming, *Philippians*, 77–78.

17. See Flemming, *Philippians*, 180–81.

18. Eshetu Abate, "Philippians," in Africa Biblical Commentary (Grand Rapids: Zondervan, 2006), 1448.

19. Flemming, *Philippians*, 249.

20. See Daniel L. Migliore, *Philippians and Philemon,* Belief: A Theological Commentary on the Bible (Louisville: Westminster John Knox, 2014), 2.

21. Flemming, *Philippians*, 30.

22. *Aegyptische Urkunden aus den Königlichen Museen zu Berlin, Griechische Urkunden* (Berlin, 1898), 2:423, in John L. White, *Light from Ancient Letters* (Philadelphia: Fortress, 1986), 159.

23. See Flemming, *Philippians*, 62.

24. For those interested in a full discussion of Paul's use of ancient rhetoric in Philippians, see Flemming, *Philippians*, 33–38.

25. Eric Metaxas, *Seven Men: And the Secret of Their Greatness* (Nashville: Nelson, 2013), xiv. See also the companion volume by the same author: *Seven Women: And the Secret of Their Greatness* (Nashville: Nelson, 2016).

26. Cotton Mather, cited in Donald A. Carson, *Basics for Believers: An Exposition of Philippians* (Grand Rapids: Baker, 1996), 94.

27. Migliore, *Philippians and Philemon*, 66.

28. See Migliore, *Philippians and Philemon*, 66.

29. I. Howard Marshall, *Philippians,* Epworth Commentaries (London: Epworth, 1991), 37.

30. Migliore, *Philippians and Philemon*, 71.

31. Alex R. G. Deasley, "Commentary on Philippians," *Illustrated Bible Life* 29 (2005): 17.

32. Some material in the following paragraphs is adapted from Flemming, *Philippians*, 92–94.

33. Migliore, *Philippians and Philemon*, 74.

34. Migliore, *Philippians and Philemon*, 75.

35. Stephen E. Fowl, *Philippians, Two Horizons New Testament Commentary* (Grand Rapids: Eerdmans, 2005), 71.

36. Ken Gire, *Windows of the Soul: Hearing God in the Everyday Moments of Your Life* (Grand Rapids: Zondervan, 1996), 181–82.

37. Some material in the following paragraphs is adapted from Flemming, *Philippians*, 99–102.

38. For a good discussion of the role of Euodia and Syntyche in relation to Paul's ministry and the Philippian church, see Cohick, *Philippians*, 209–11.

39. Dietrich Bonhoeffer, *Life Together*, trans. J. W. Doberstein (New York: Harper & Row, 1954), 25–26.

40. This section adapts material from Flemming, *Philippians*, 206–7.

41. Flemming, *Philippians*, 207.

42. Migliore, *Philippians and Philemon*, 81.

43. Eugene Peterson, *Eat This Book: A Conversation in the Art of Spiritual Reading* (Grand Rapids: Eerdmans, 2006), 43. Peterson makes this observation about Scripture's approach as a whole.

44. This section adapts some material from Flemming, *Philippians*, 125–26.

45. Dallas Willard, *The Divine Conspiracy: Rediscovering Our Hidden Life in God* (San Francisco: HarperSanFrancisco, 1988), 183.

46. A version of this story appears in Dean Flemming, *Recovering the Full Mission of God: A Biblical Perspective on Being, Doing, and Telling* (Downers Grove, IL: IVP Academic, 2013), 183.

47. See Flemming, *Philippians*, 131.

48. Flemming, *Recovering the Full Mission of God*, 192.

49. Cited from Dean Flemming, *Why Mission?* (Nashville: Abingdon, 2015).

50. For arguments in favor of this translation, see James P. Ware, *Paul and the Mission of the Church: Philippians in Ancient Jewish Context* (Grand Rapids: Baker Academic, 2011), 256–70, 283–84.

51. Michael J. Gorman, *Becoming the Gospel: Paul, Participation, and Mission* (Grand Rapids: Eerdmans, 2015), 127.

52. See Flemming, *Philippians*, 223.

53. Gorman, *Apostle of the Crucified Lord*, 446.

54. See Cohick, *Philippians*, 227.

55. Flemming, *Philippians*, 52.

56. Migliore, *Philippians and Philemon*, 159.

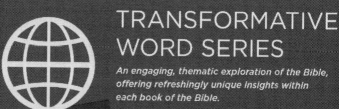